12 Notes

BIG KEYBOARD AND PIANO CHORD BOOK

By Richard Moran

12 Notes - Big Keyboard and Piano Chord Book
Edition I

www.MoranEducation.com/12Notes

ISBN 978-1-4710-1495-6

Introduction | Our Chord Diagrams Explained

The Big Keyboard and Piano Chord Book presents over 500 keyboard and piano chords in our unique easy to read format. With large clear and concise diagrams, we show you all the keyboard chords you'll ever need to know.

Get started by finding the chord you wish to play.

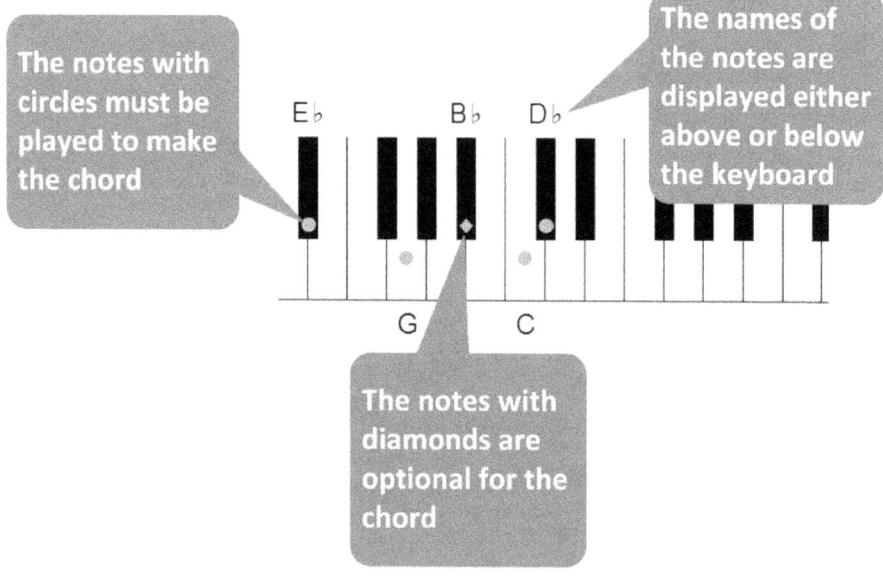

The names of the notes are displayed either above or below the keyboard

The notes with circles must be played to make the chord

The notes with diamonds are optional for the chord

Introduction

Here, we've given you some background on how the keyboard is laid out. Don't worry if this is all new to you. It's good to know, but not necessary to use the book.

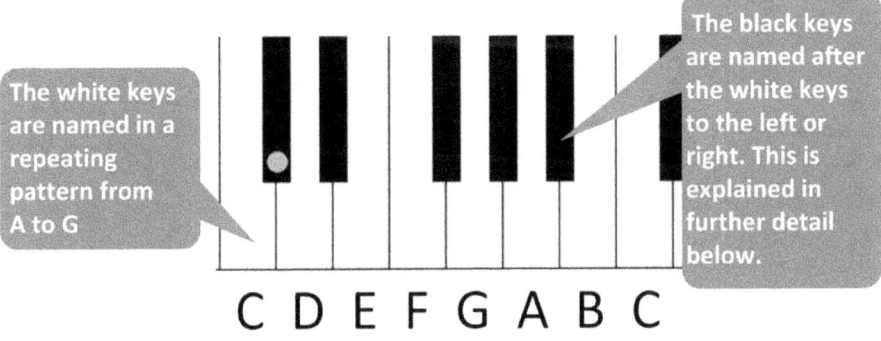

The white keys are named in a repeating pattern from A to G

The black keys are named after the white keys to the left or right. This is explained in further detail below.

C D E F G A B C

For instance, to find a 'C' on the keyboard, look for the black notes in a group of two, and play the white note immediately to the left of the group.

To play a 'B', look for the black notes in a group of three, and play the note immediately to the right of the group.

The black keys are represented by a sharp (#) or flat (♭) sign.
A sharp sign tells you to play the note immediately to the right of the named white note.

A flat sign tells you to play the note immediately to the left of the named white note.

For example, we've highlighted C# in the picture above. We've also highlighted D ♭ - it's exactly the same note!

Introduction | More about Chords

When there are many sharps and flats in the chord, sometimes we use double sharps (represented by an 'x' and double flats (represented by two flat signs).

A double sharp tells you to count up two keys on the keyboard (e.g. Cx is the same note as D).

A double flat tells you to count down two keys on the keyboard (e.g. D ♭♭ is the same note as C).

Quick tips:

Is your chord not listed in the book? Remember that...

A ♭ can also be written as G#
B ♭ can also be written as A#
C# can also be written as D ♭
E ♭ can also be written as D#
F# can also be written as G ♭

... so if the given chord is D ♭ maj7, substitute C#maj7 instead.. it's actually exactly the same chord!

Introduction

Other chord naming conventions:

There are multiple naming conventions for chords. We've used the most popular versions in our book. In case you encounter any other ways of writing these chords, we've put together a quick guide below...

In these examples, we've substituted 'X' for the first letter of the chord.

Major Chords - These are sometimes written as XMaj, XM, or just 'X'

Minor Chords - Are sometimes written as Xmin or Xmi. We use Xm.

Chords with a '-' sign in them are also sometimes written with a ' ♭ ' instead

Chords with a '+' sign in them are also sometimes written with a '#' instead

Diminished Seventh Chords are shown as a 'X°'. They can also be written as X°7, Xdim7, X-7, and Xdim

Suspended Chords - 'sus' chords can also be written as 'sus4'

'7sus', 'sus7', and '7sus4' are all exactly the same.

Augmented chords can be written as '+', '#5', '+5', or 'aug'

Major Sixth chords can be written as '6', 'Maj6, or 'M6'

Major Sixth add Nine can be written as '6/9, 6(add9'), 'Maj6(add9)', or 'M6(add9)'

'X7' is sometimes written as 'X Dom 7'

Chords

A♭ is also known as G#

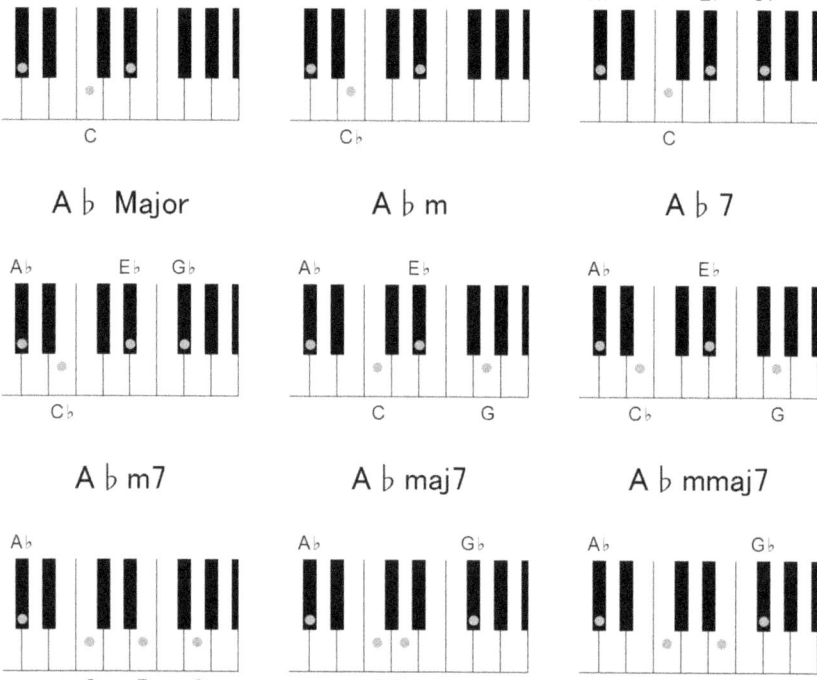

A♭ Major	A♭ m	A♭ 7
A♭ m7	A♭ maj7	A♭ mmaj7
A♭ maj7+5	A♭ 7-5	A♭ 7+5

Big Keyboard and Piano Chord Book
©2011 Moran Education http://www.MoranEducation.com/12Notes

A♭

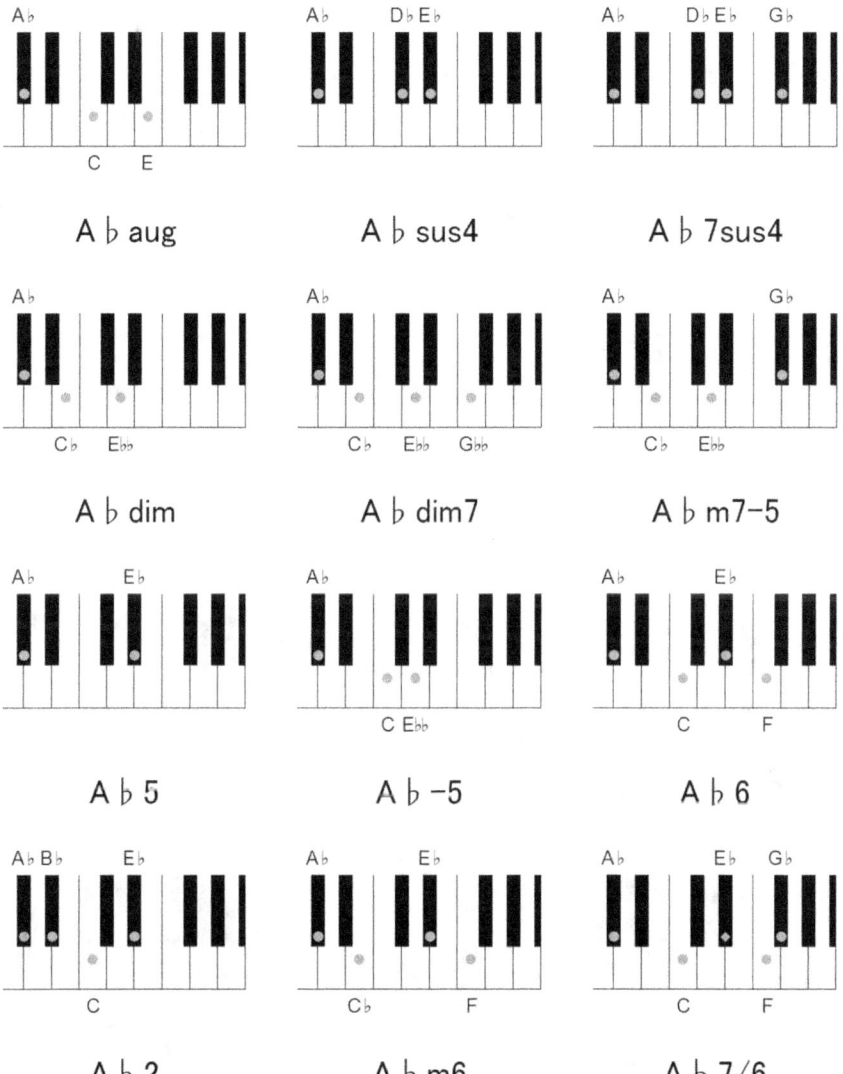

A♭ aug

A♭ sus4

A♭ 7sus4

A♭ dim

A♭ dim7

A♭ m7−5

A♭ 5

A♭ −5

A♭ 6

A♭ 2

A♭ m6

A♭ 7/6

Chords

A♭ | *Continued*

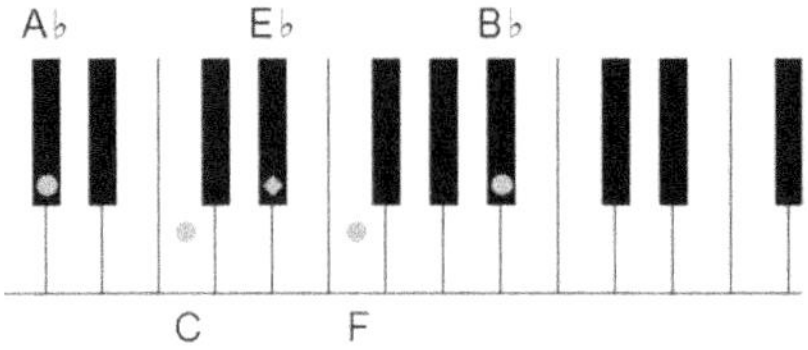

A♭ 6/9

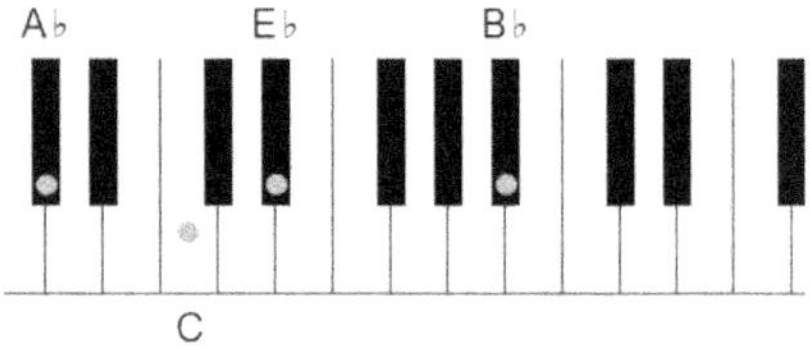

A♭ add9

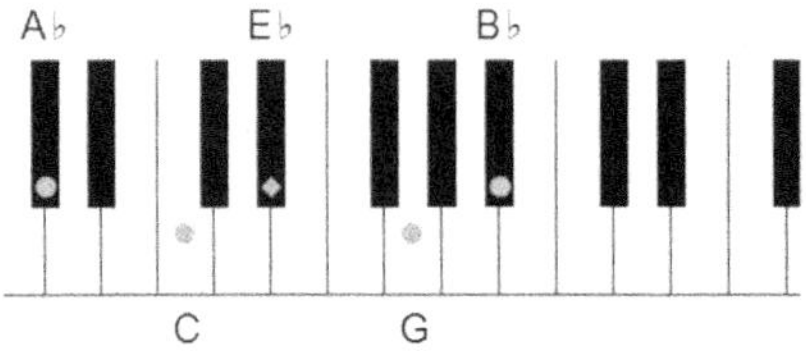

A♭ maj9

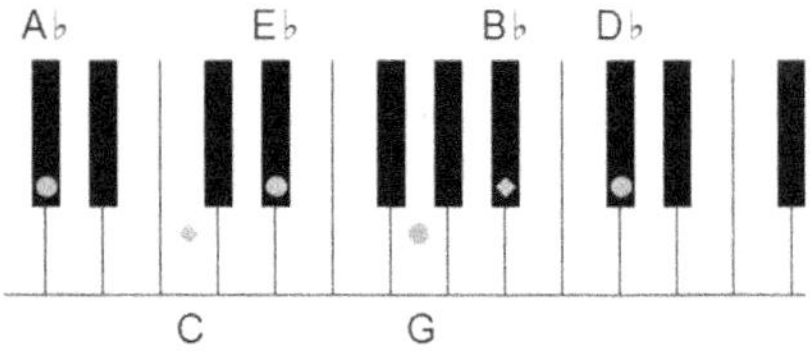

A♭ maj11

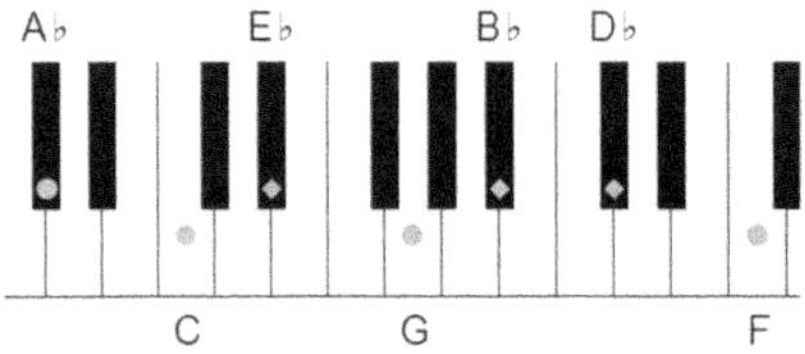

A♭ maj13

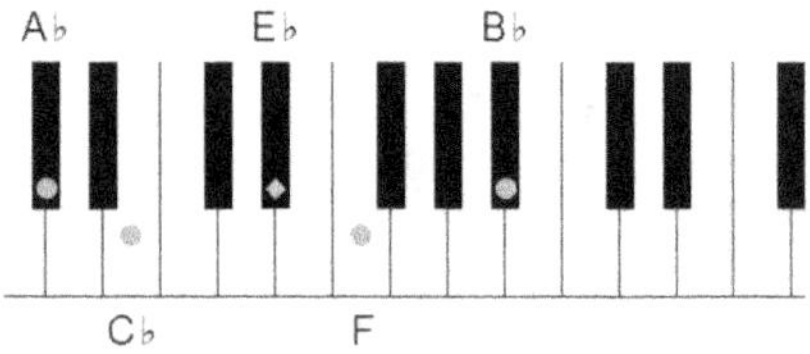

A♭ m6/9

Big Keyboard and Piano Chord Book

©2011 Moran Education http://www.MoranEducation.com/12Notes

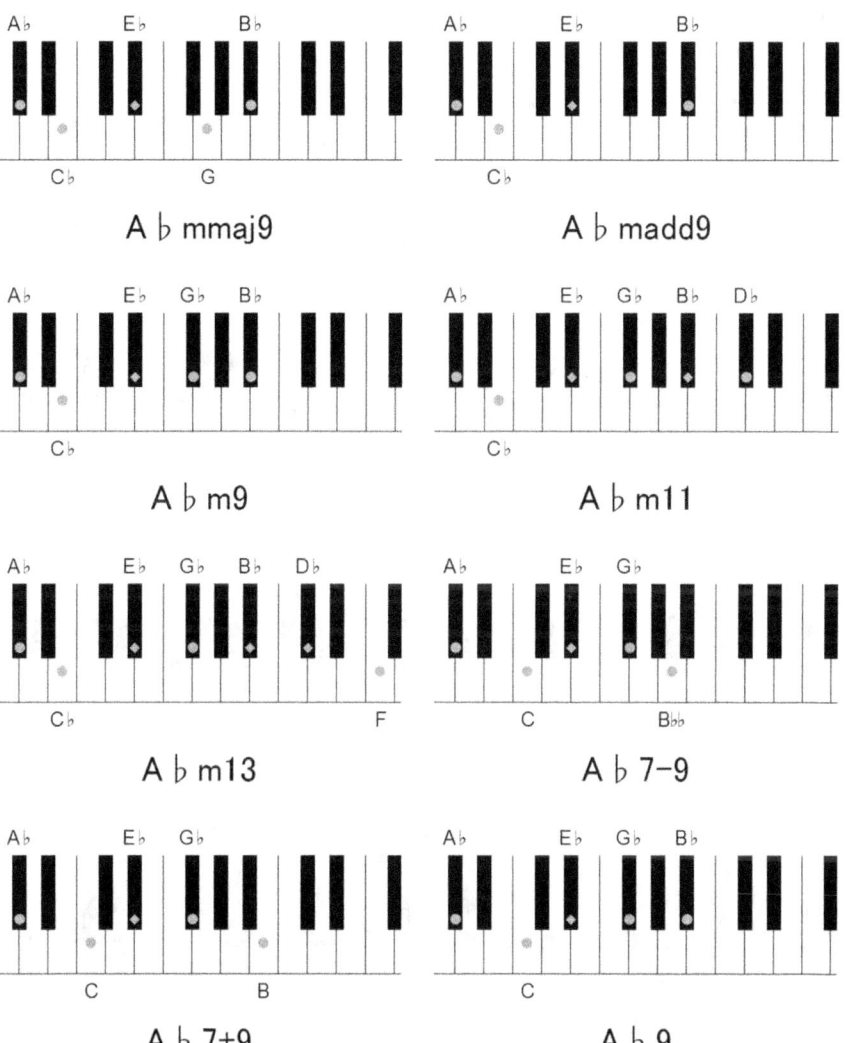

A♭ mmaj9

A♭ madd9

A♭ m9

A♭ m11

A♭ m13

A♭ 7-9

A♭ 7+9

A♭ 9

Chords | *Continued*

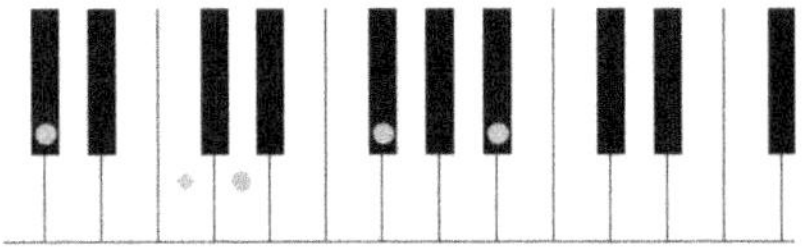

A♭ 9−5

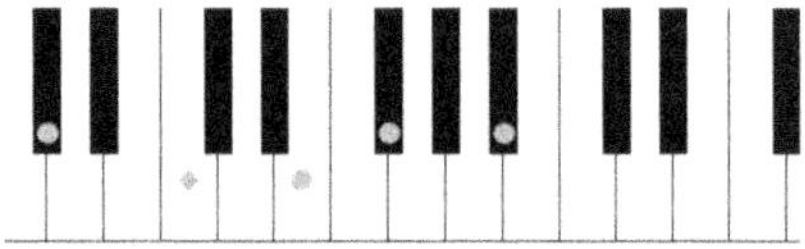

A♭ 9+5

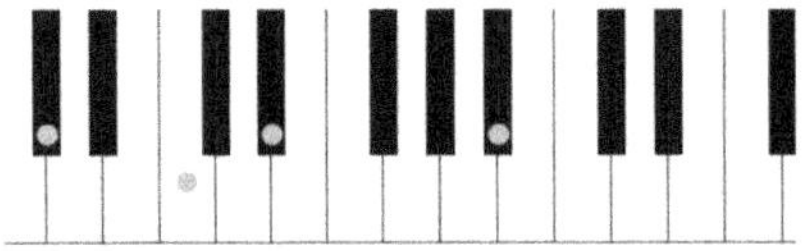

A♭ add9

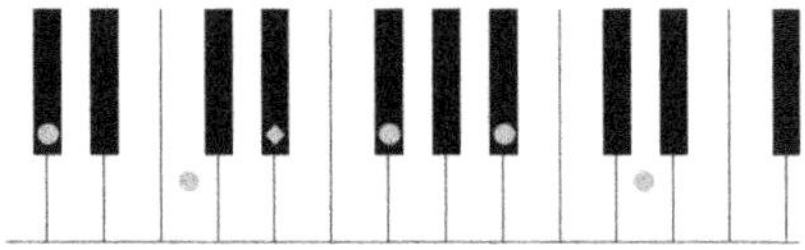

A♭ 9+11

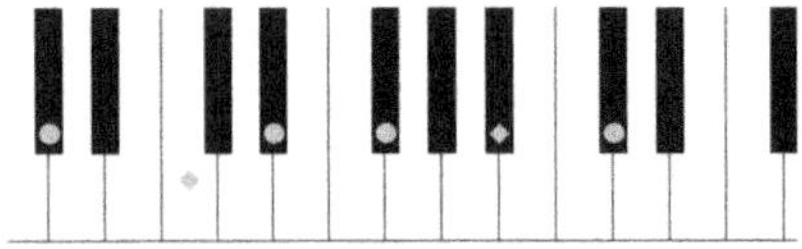

A♭ 11

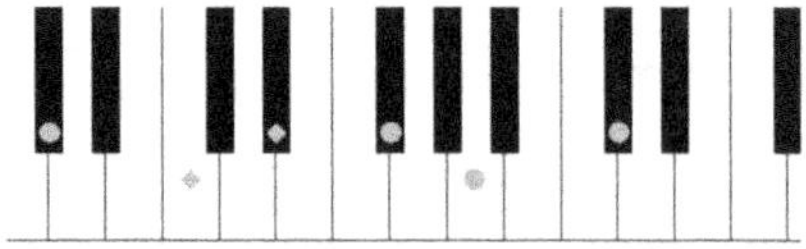

A♭ 11−9

Big Keyboard and Piano Chord Book
©2011 Moran Education http://www.MoranEducation.com/12Notes

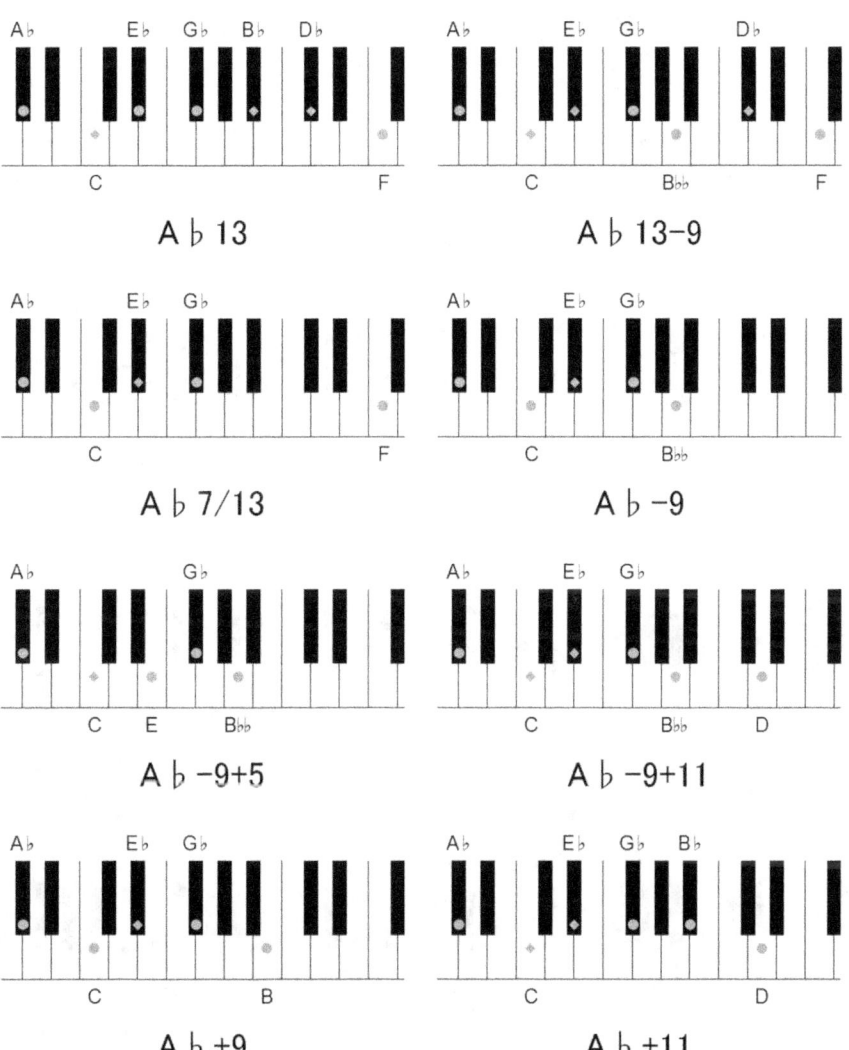

A♭ 13

A♭ 13-9

A♭ 7/13

A♭ -9

A♭ -9+5

A♭ -9+11

A♭ +9

A♭ +11

A
Chords

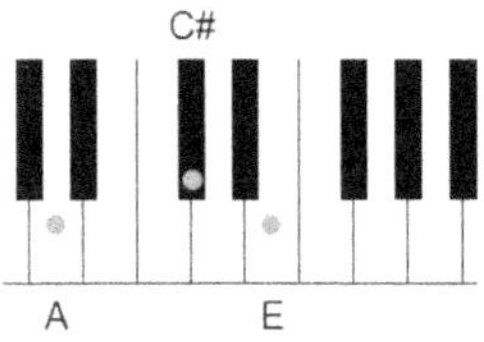

C#		C#
A Major	Am	A7

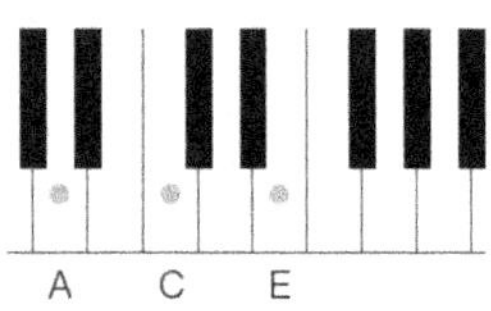

Am /	Amaj7	Ammaj7

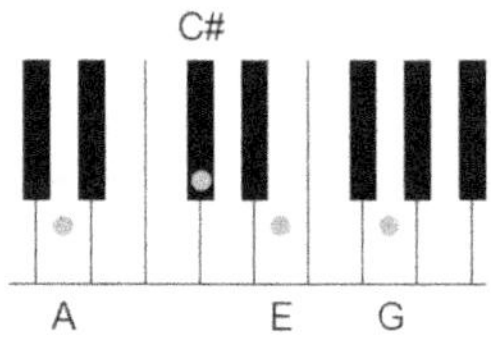

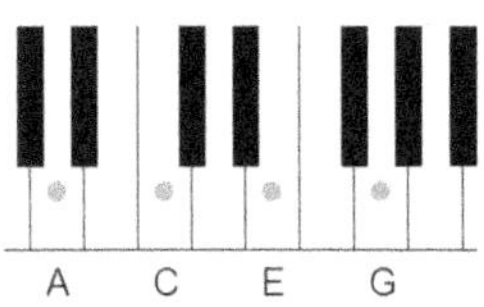

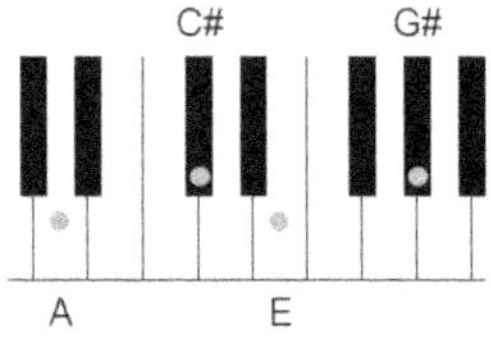

Amaj7+5	A7-5	A7+5

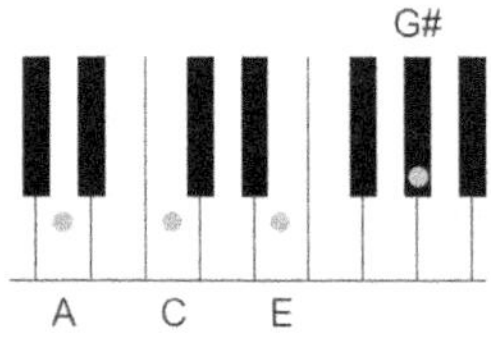

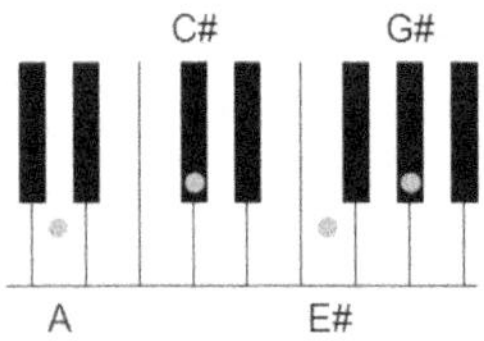

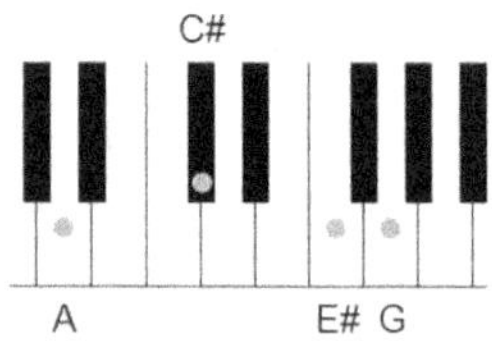

Big Keyboard and Piano Chord Book

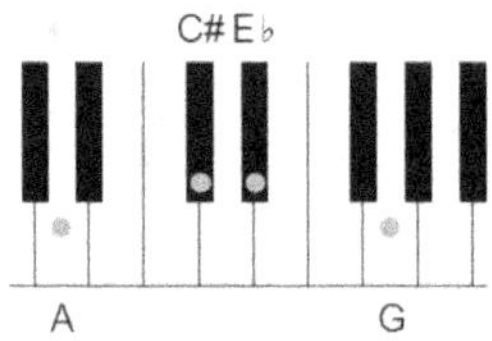

©2011 Moran Education http://www.MoranEducation.com/12Notes

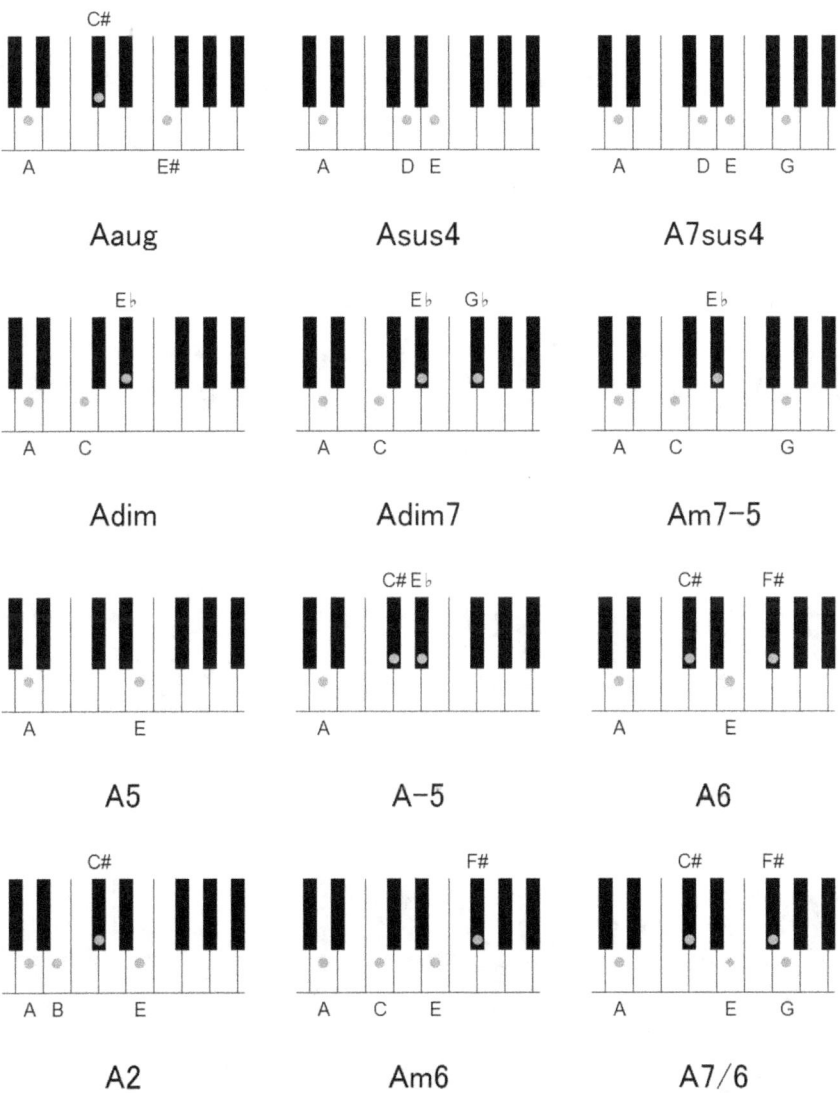

Aaug

Asus4

A7sus4

Adim

Adim7

Am7−5

A5

A−5

A6

A2

Am6

A7/6

A Chords

Continued

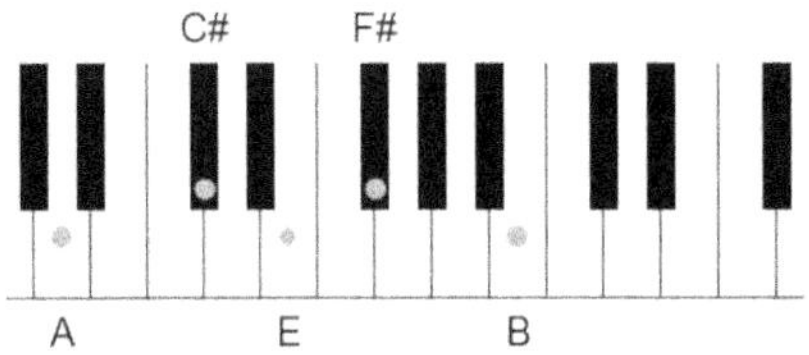

C# F#

A   E   B

A6/9

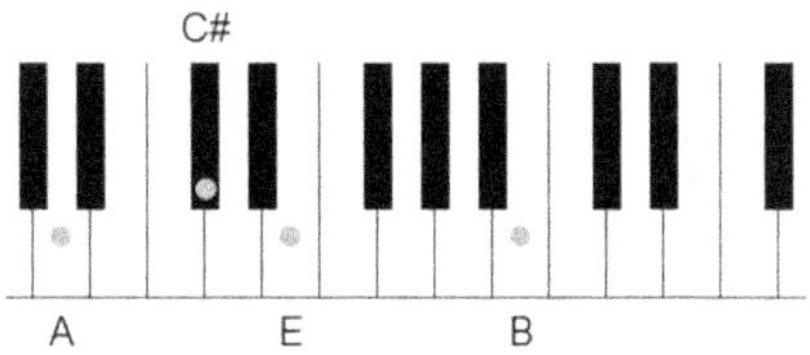

C#

A   E   B

Aadd9

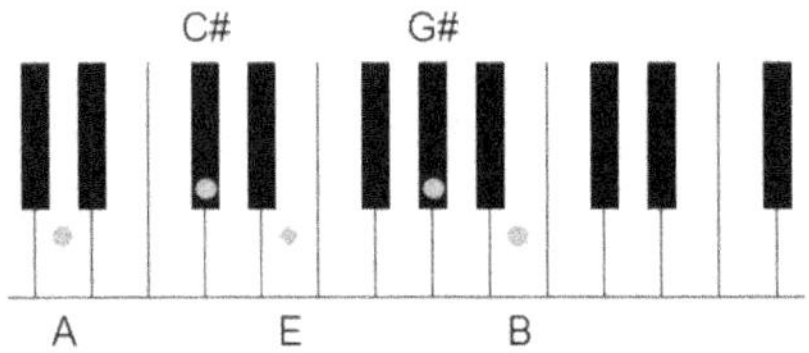

C# G#

A   E   B

Amaj9

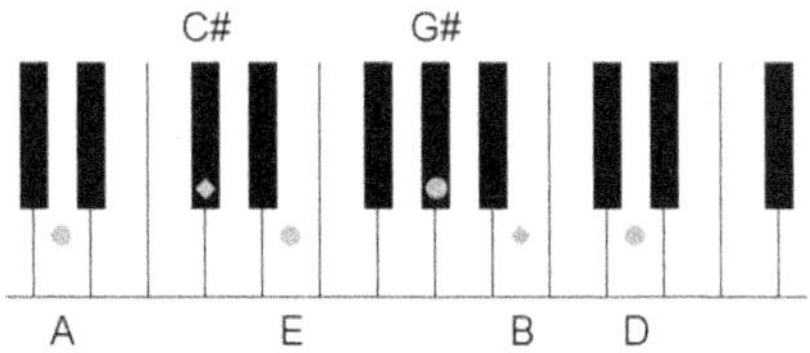

C# G#

A   E   B   D

Amaj11

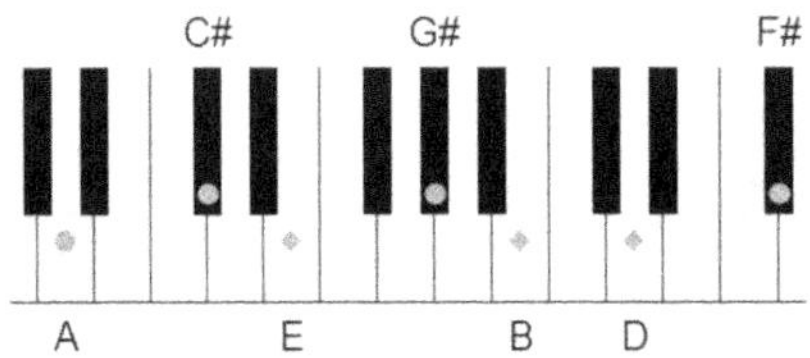

C# G# F#

A   E   B   D

Amaj13

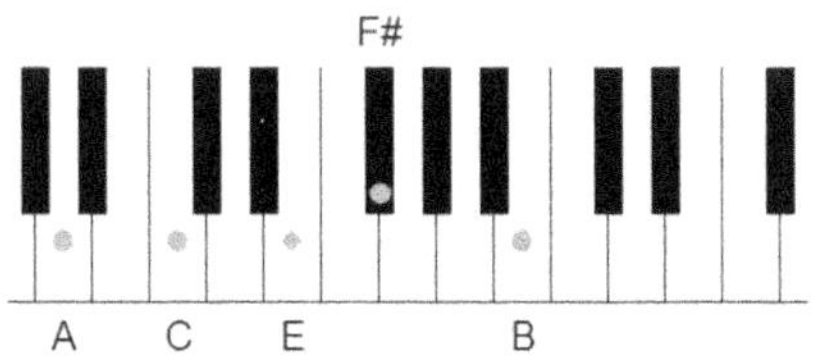

F#

A   C   E   B

Am6/9

Big Keyboard and Piano Chord Book
©2011 Moran Education http://www.MoranEducation.com/12Notes

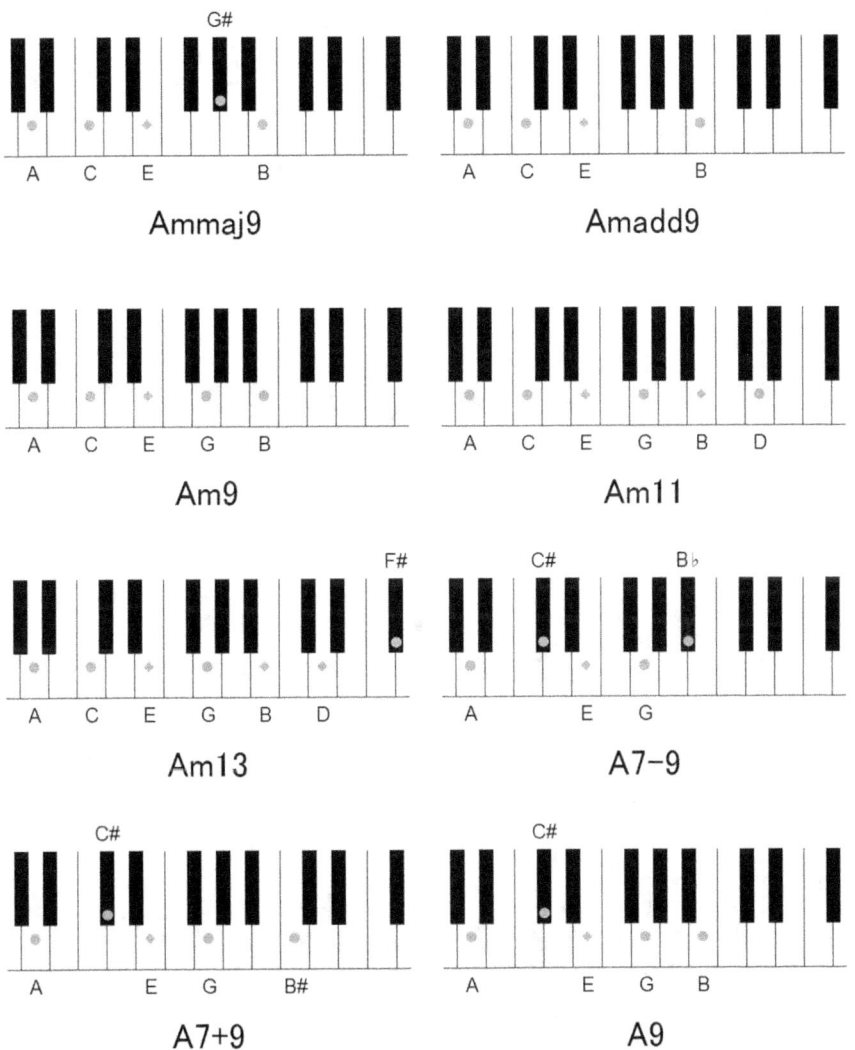

Ammaj9

Amadd9

Am9

Am11

Am13

A7−9

A7+9

A9

A

Chords

Continued

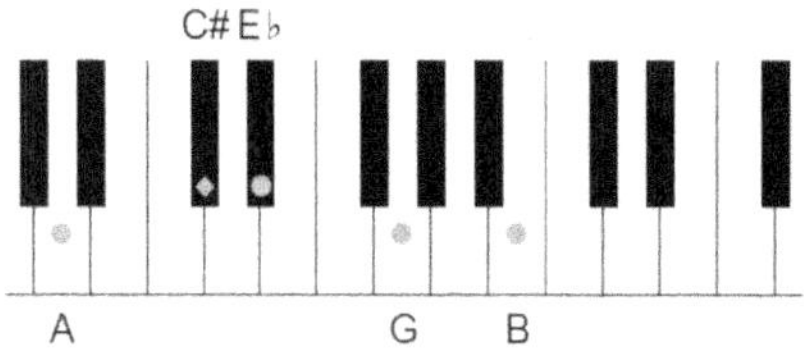

A9−5

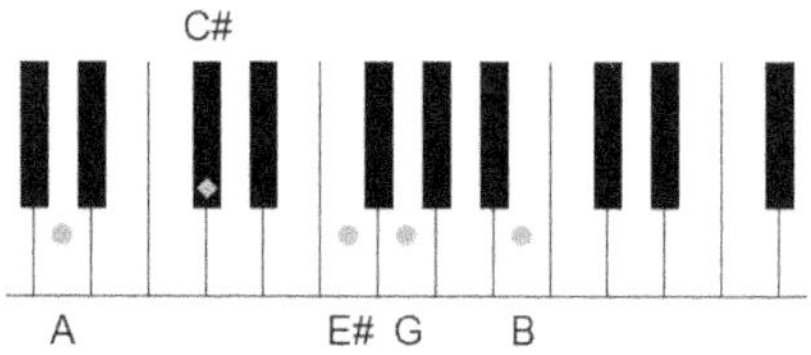

C# E♭

A   G   B

A9+5

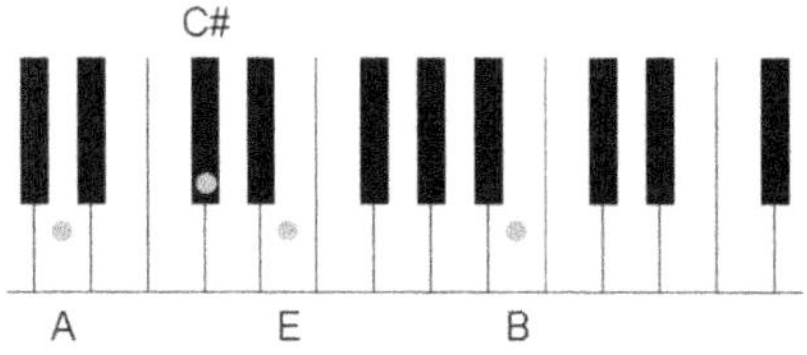

C#

A   E# G   B

Aadd9

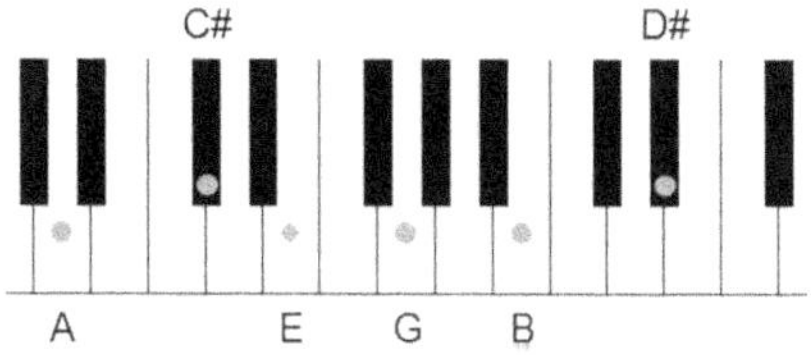

C#

A   E   B

A9+11

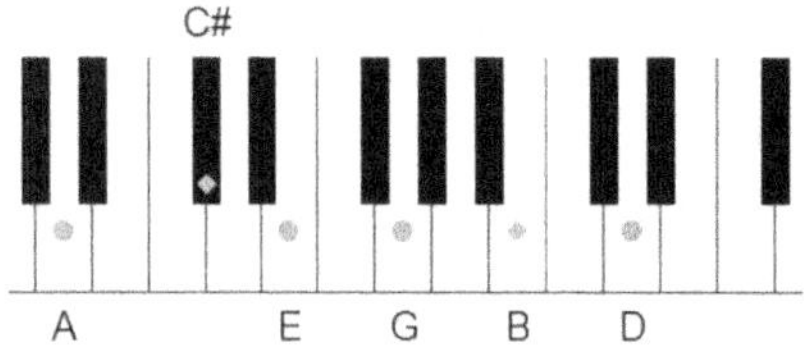

C#   D#

A   E   G   B

A11

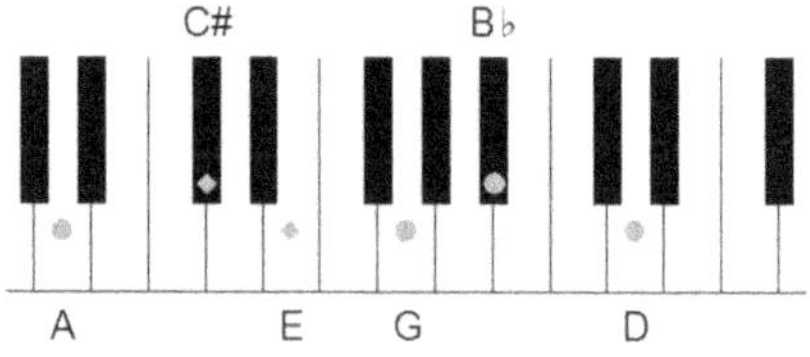

C#

A   E   G   B   D

A11−9

C#   B♭

A   E   G   D

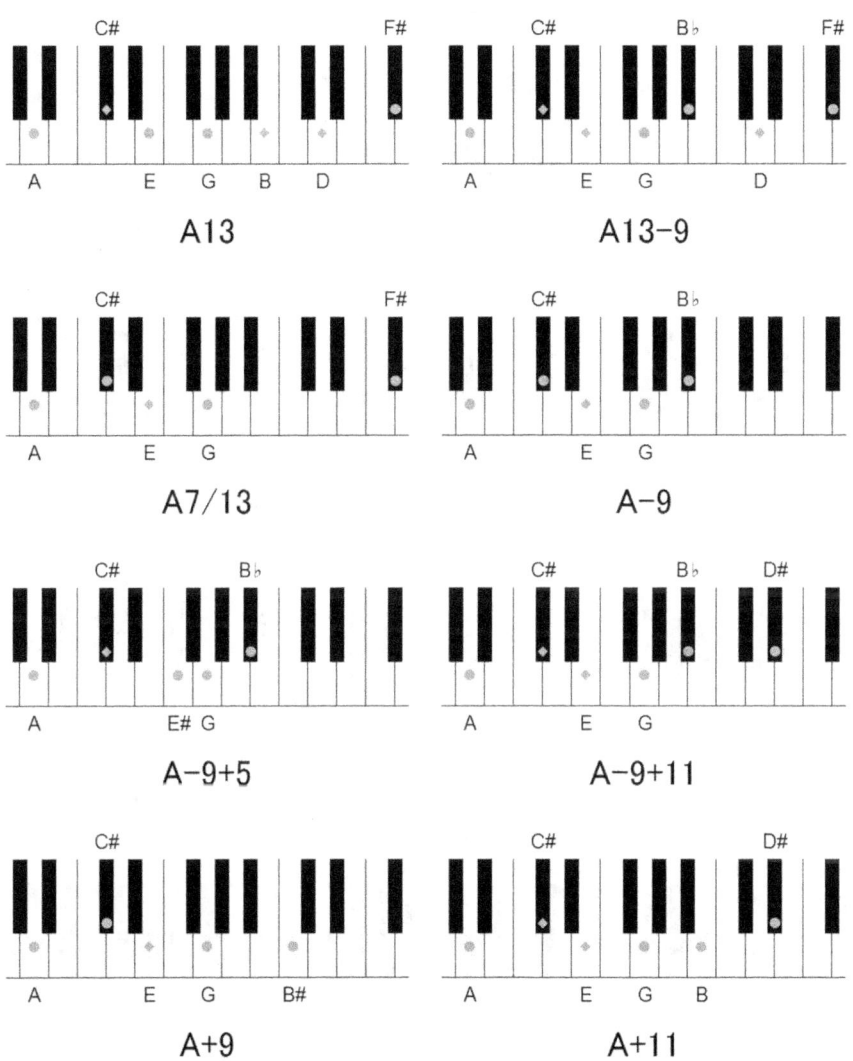

A13

A13-9

A7/13

A-9

A-9+5

A-9+11

A+9

A+11

B♭

B♭ is also known as A#

Chords

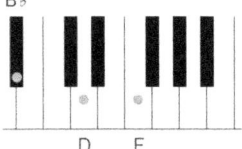

B♭ Major

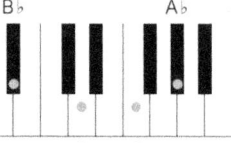

B♭m

B♭7

B♭m7

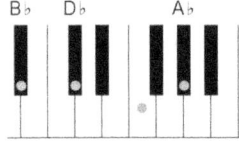

B♭maj7

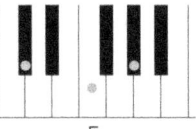

B♭mmaj7

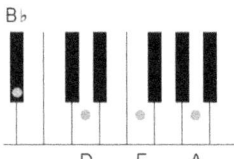

B♭maj7+5

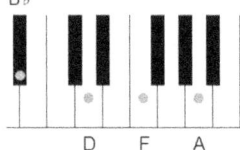

B♭7-5

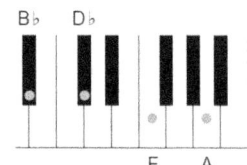

B♭7+5

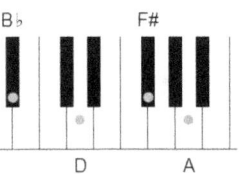

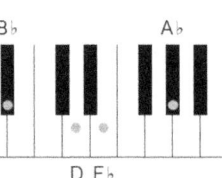

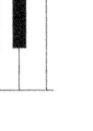

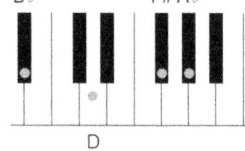

B♭

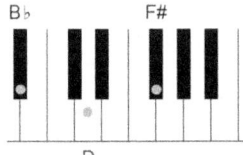

B♭ aug

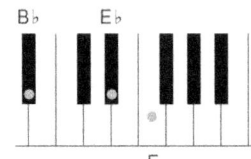

B♭ sus4

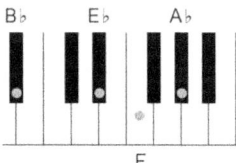

B♭ 7sus4

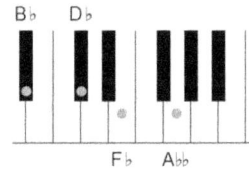

B♭ dim

B♭ dim7

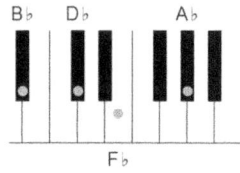

B♭ m7-5

B♭ 5

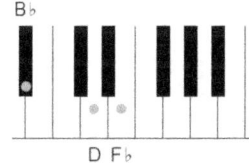

B♭ -5

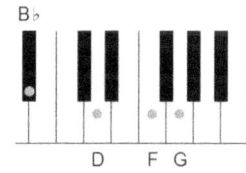

B♭ 6

B♭ 2

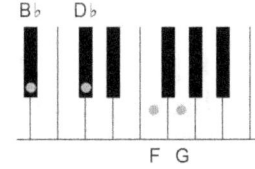

B♭ m6

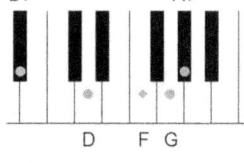

B♭ 7/6

B♭

Continued

Chords

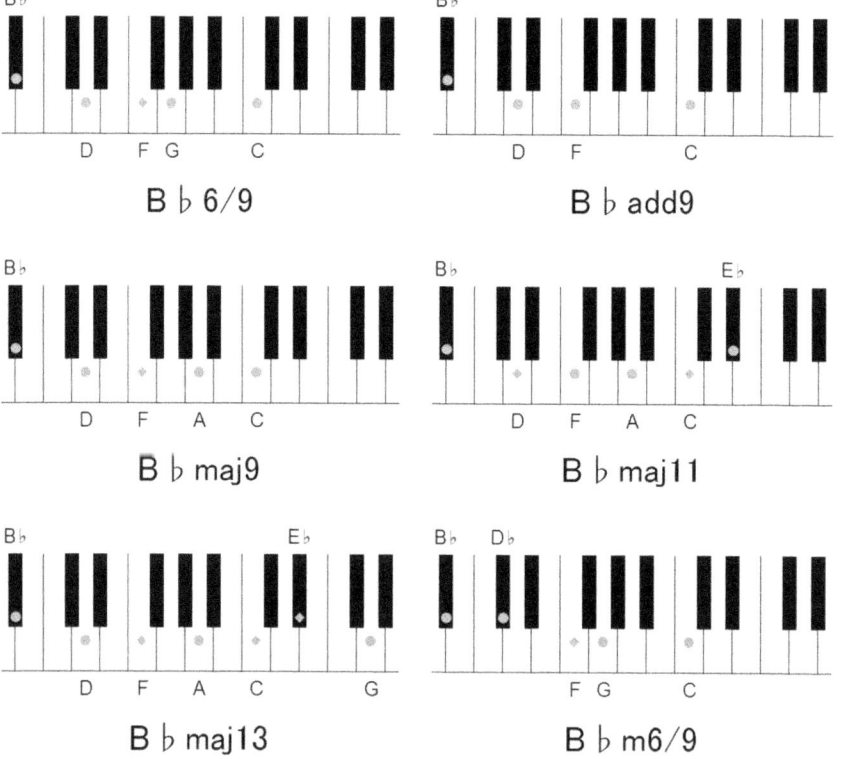

B♭ 6/9

B♭ add9

B♭ maj9

B♭ maj11

B♭ maj13

B♭ m6/9

B♭

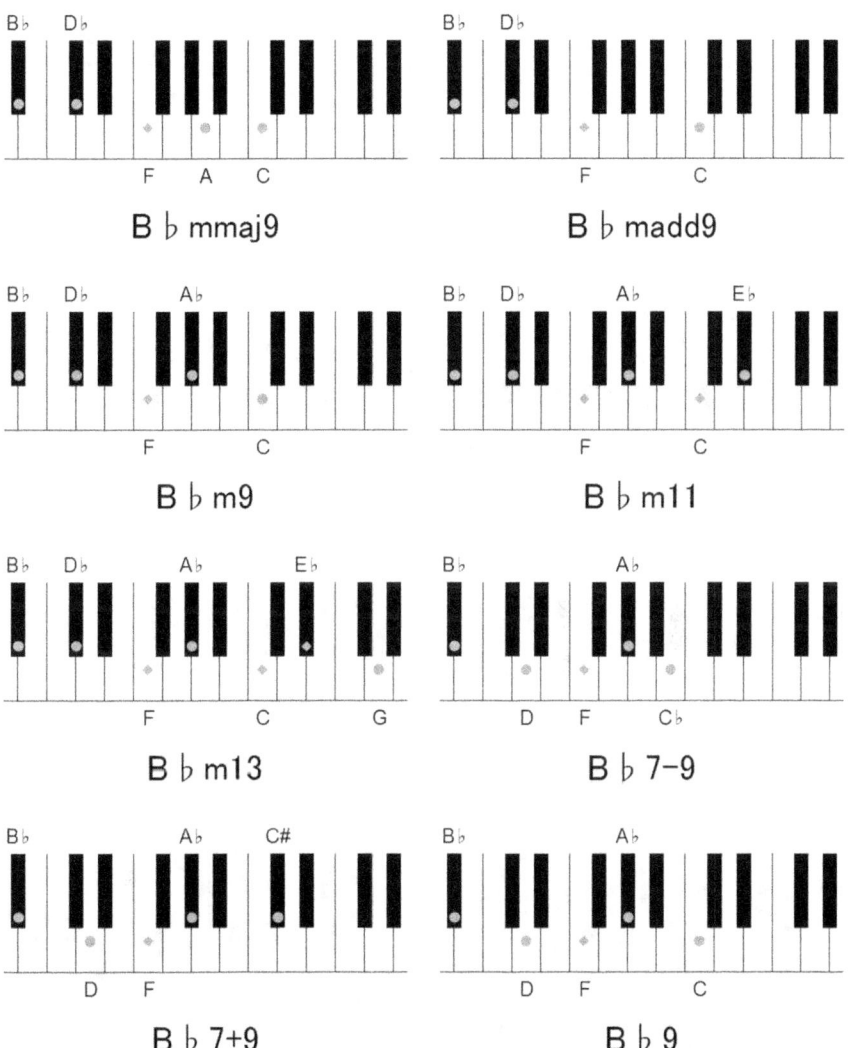

B♭ mmaj9

B♭ madd9

B♭ m9

B♭ m11

B♭ m13

B♭ 7-9

B♭ 7+9

B♭ 9

B♭ Chords

Continued

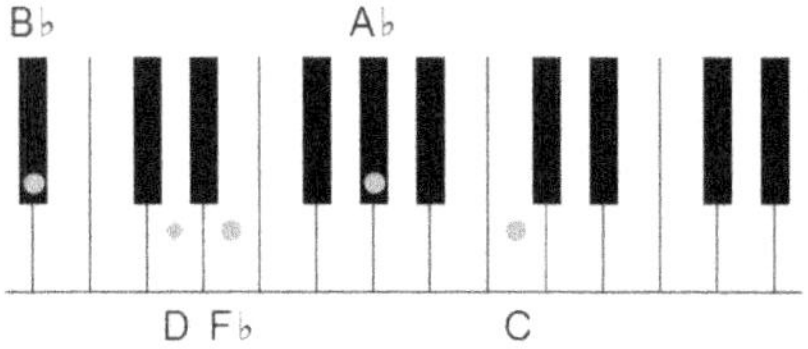

B♭9-5

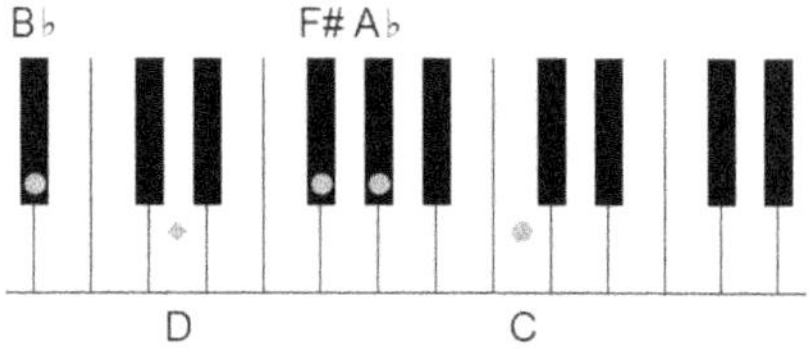

B♭9+5

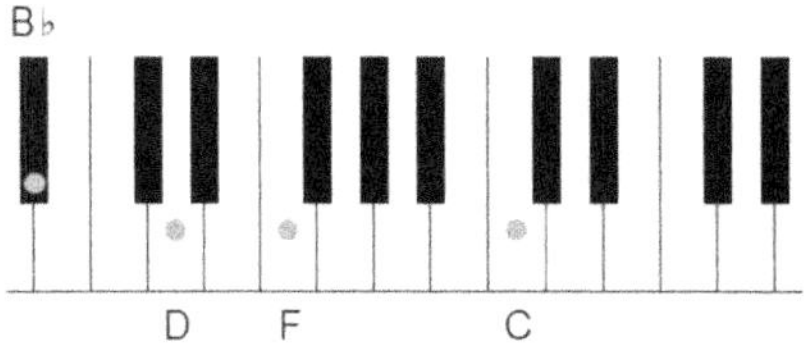

B♭add9

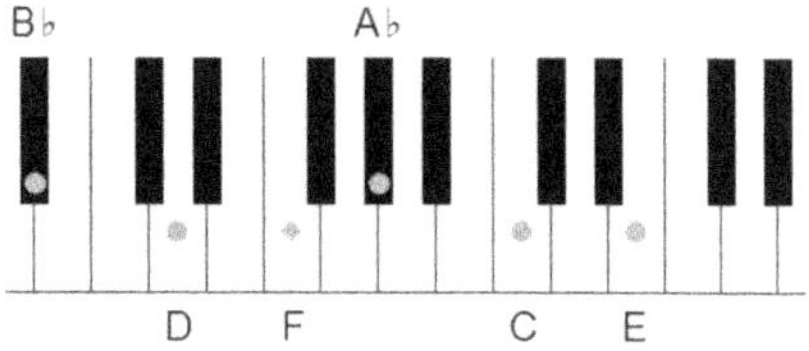

B♭9+11

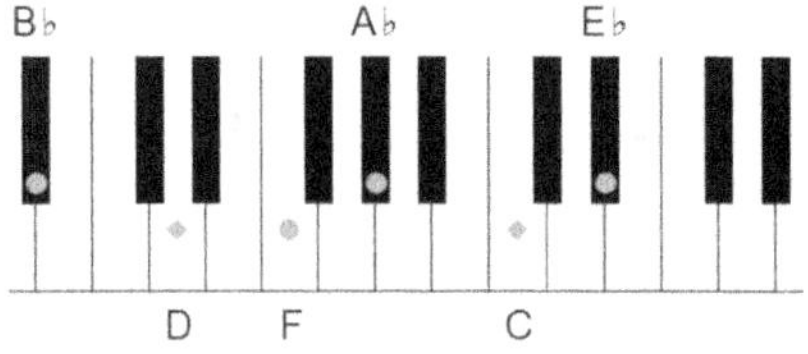

B♭11

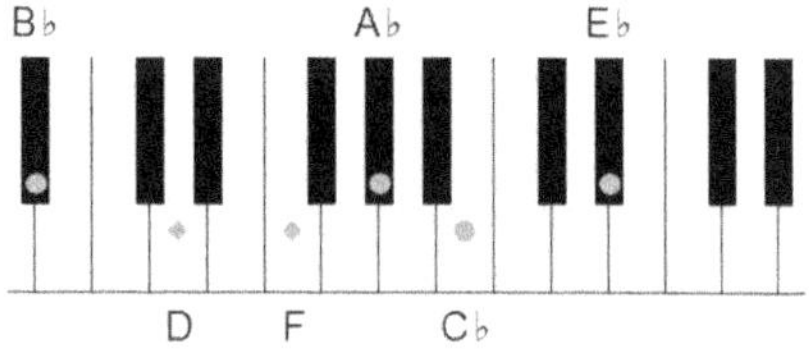

B♭11-9

Big Keyboard and Piano Chord Book

©2011 Moran Education http://www.MoranEducation.com/12Notes

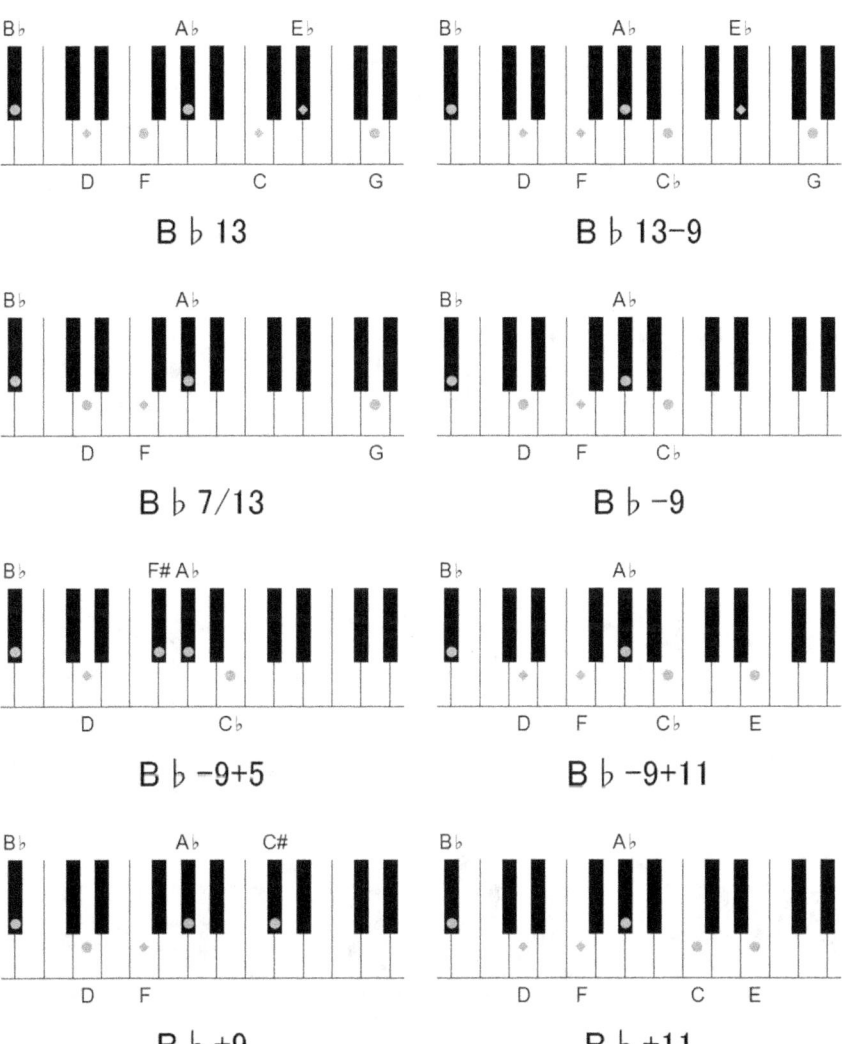

B ♭ 13

B ♭ 13-9

B ♭ 7/13

B ♭ -9

B ♭ -9+5

B ♭ -9+11

B ♭ +9

B ♭ +11

B

Chords

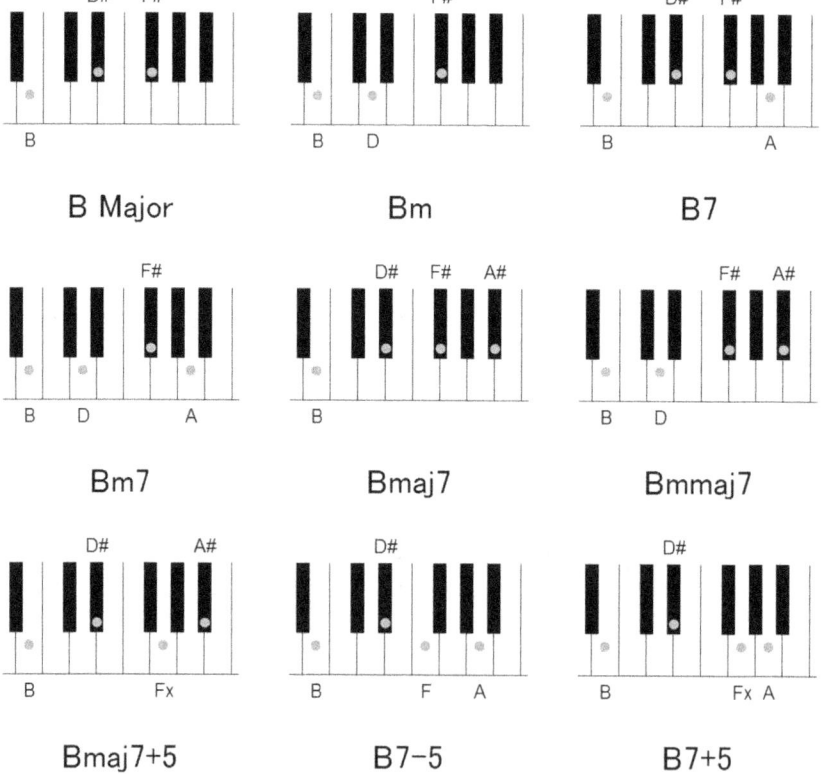

B Major

Bm

B7

Bm7

Bmaj7

Bmmaj7

Bmaj7+5

B7-5

B7+5

Big Keyboard and Piano Chord Book
©2011 Moran Education http://www.MoranEducation.com/12Notes

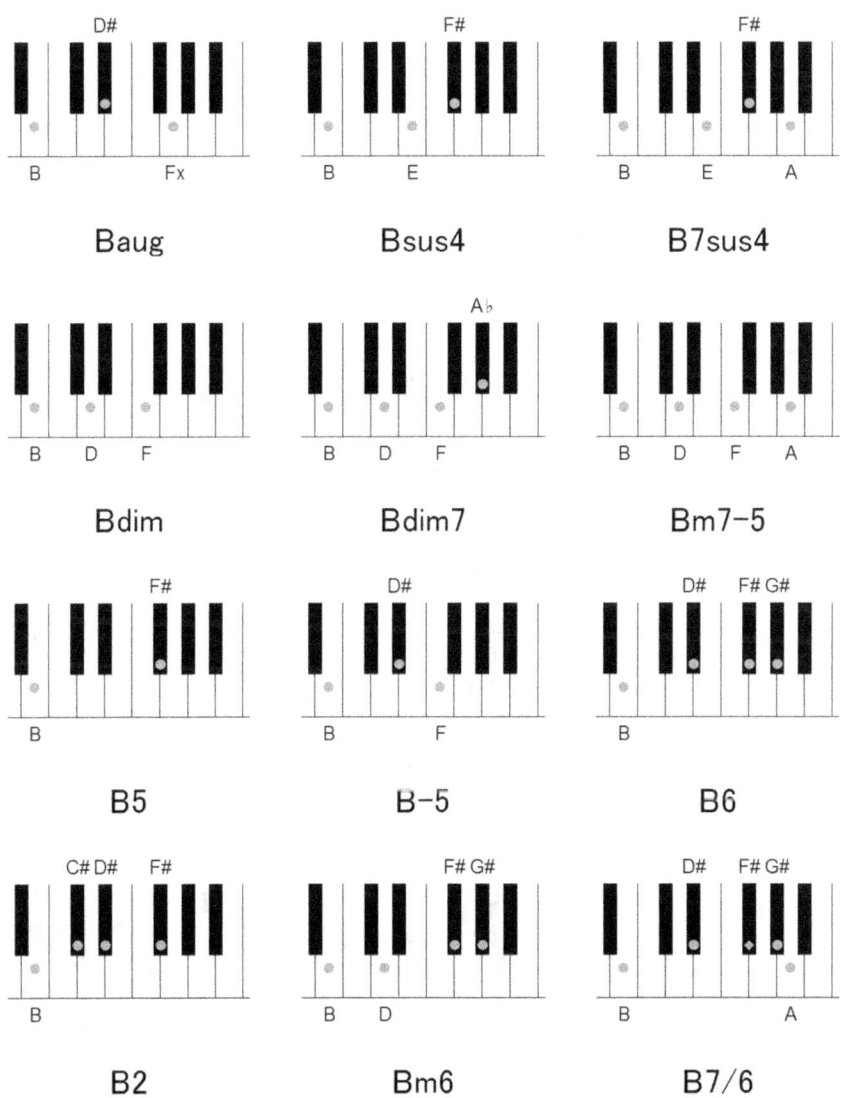

D#

B   Fx

Baug

F#

B   E

Bsus4

F#

B   E   A

B7sus4

B   D   F

Bdim

Ab

B   D   F

Bdim7

B   D   F   A

Bm7−5

F#

B

B5

D#

B   F

B−5

D#   F# G#

B

B6

C# D#   F#

B

B2

F# G#

B   D

Bm6

D#   F# G#

B   A

B7/6

B
Chords

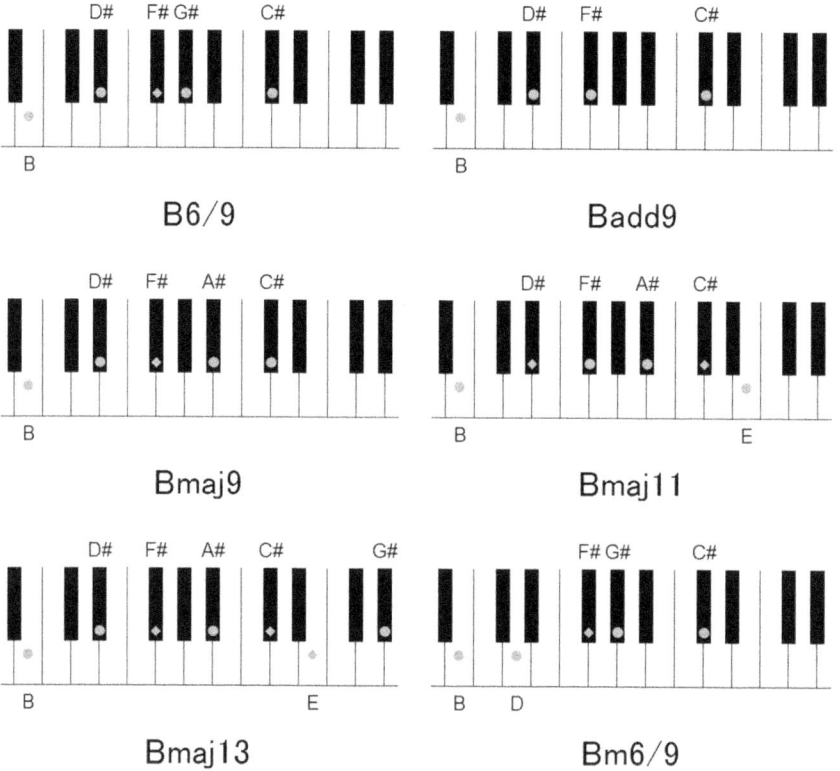

B6/9

Badd9

Bmaj9

Bmaj11

Bmaj13

Bm6/9

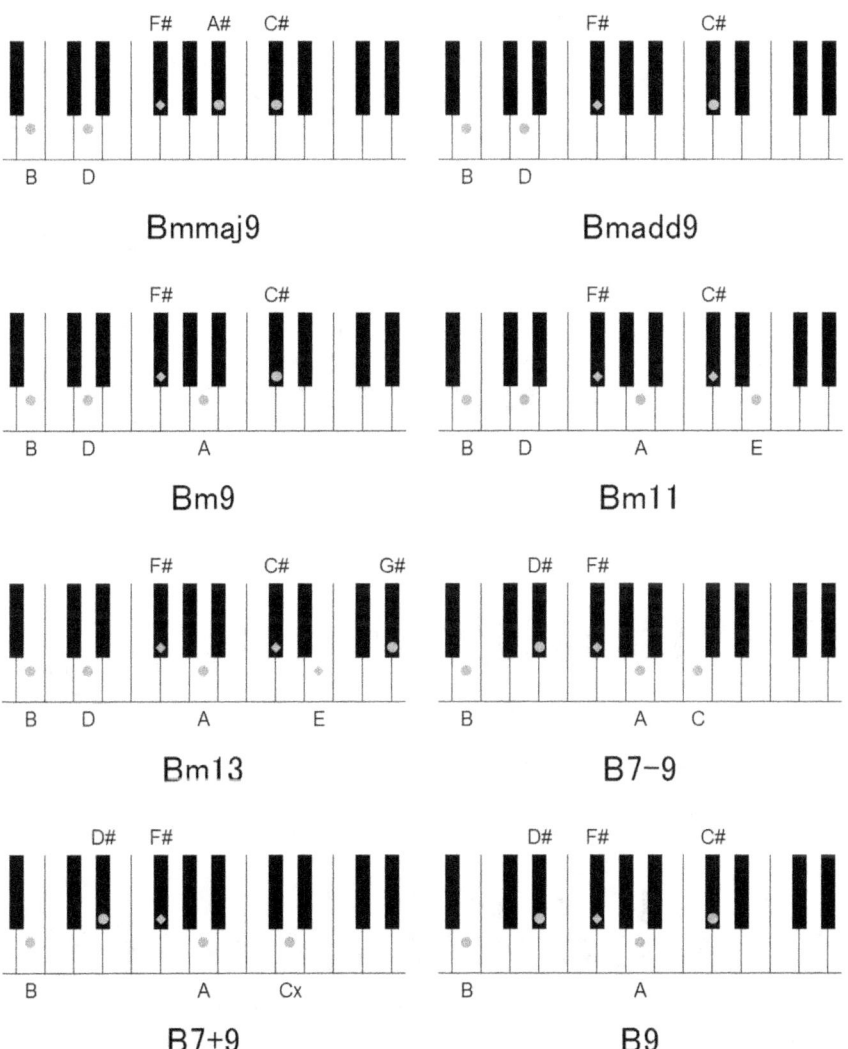

Bmmaj9

Bmadd9

Bm9

Bm11

Bm13

B7−9

B7+9

B9

B

Continued

Chords

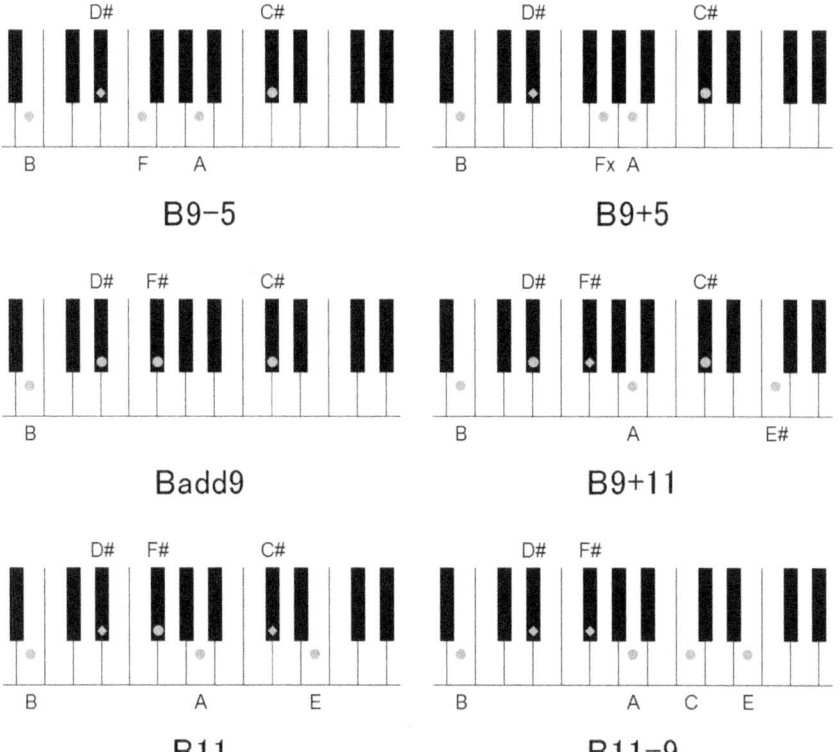

B9-5

B9+5

Badd9

B9+11

B11

B11-9

Big Keyboard and Piano Chord Book

©2011 Moran Education http://www.MoranEducation.com/12Notes

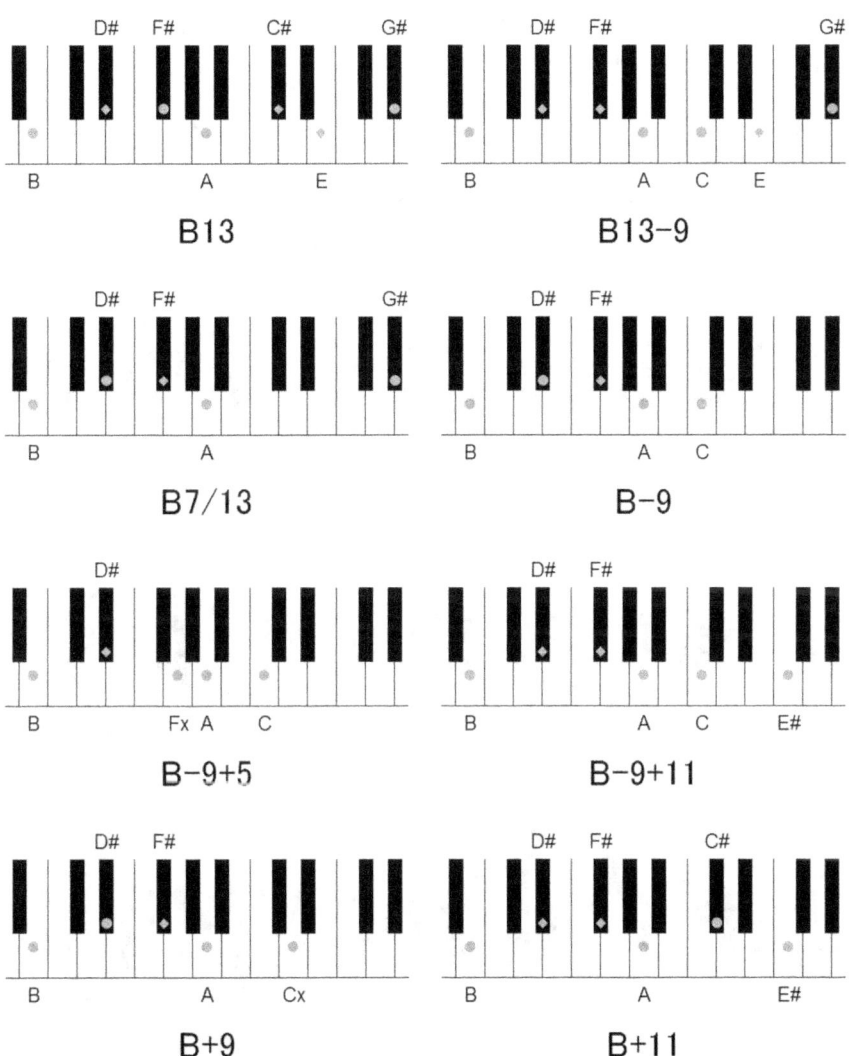

B13

B13-9

B7/13

B-9

B-9+5

B-9+11

B+9

B+11

C

Chords

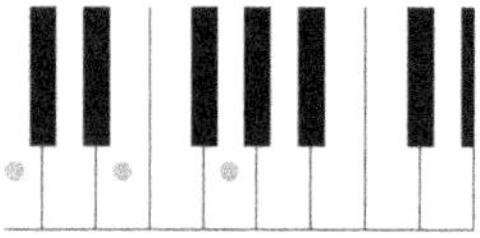

C Major	**Cm**	**C7**
C E G	C (Eb) G	C E G D
Cm7	**Cmaj7**	**Cmmaj7**
C (Eb) G (Bb)	C E G B	C (Eb) G B
Cmaj7+5	**C7−5**	**C7+5**
C E (G#) B	C E (Gb) (Bb)	C E (G#)(Bb)

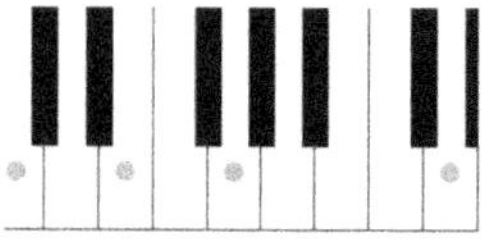

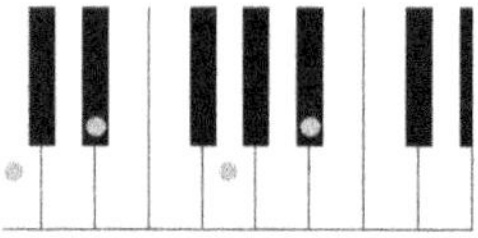

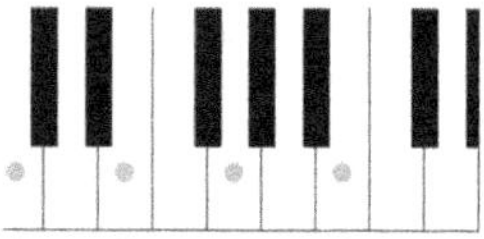

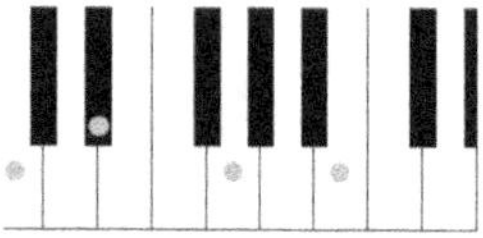

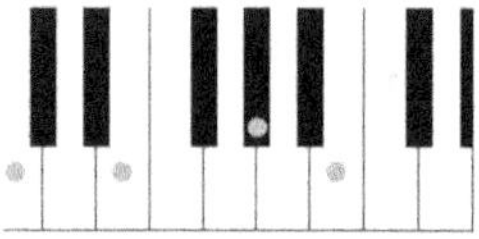

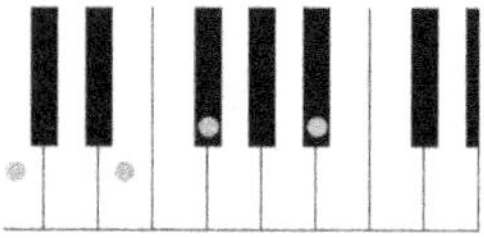

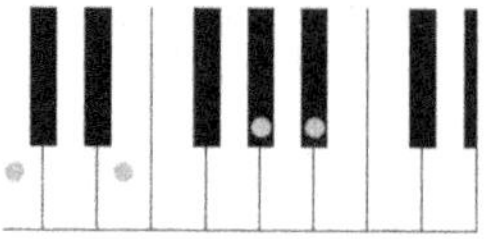

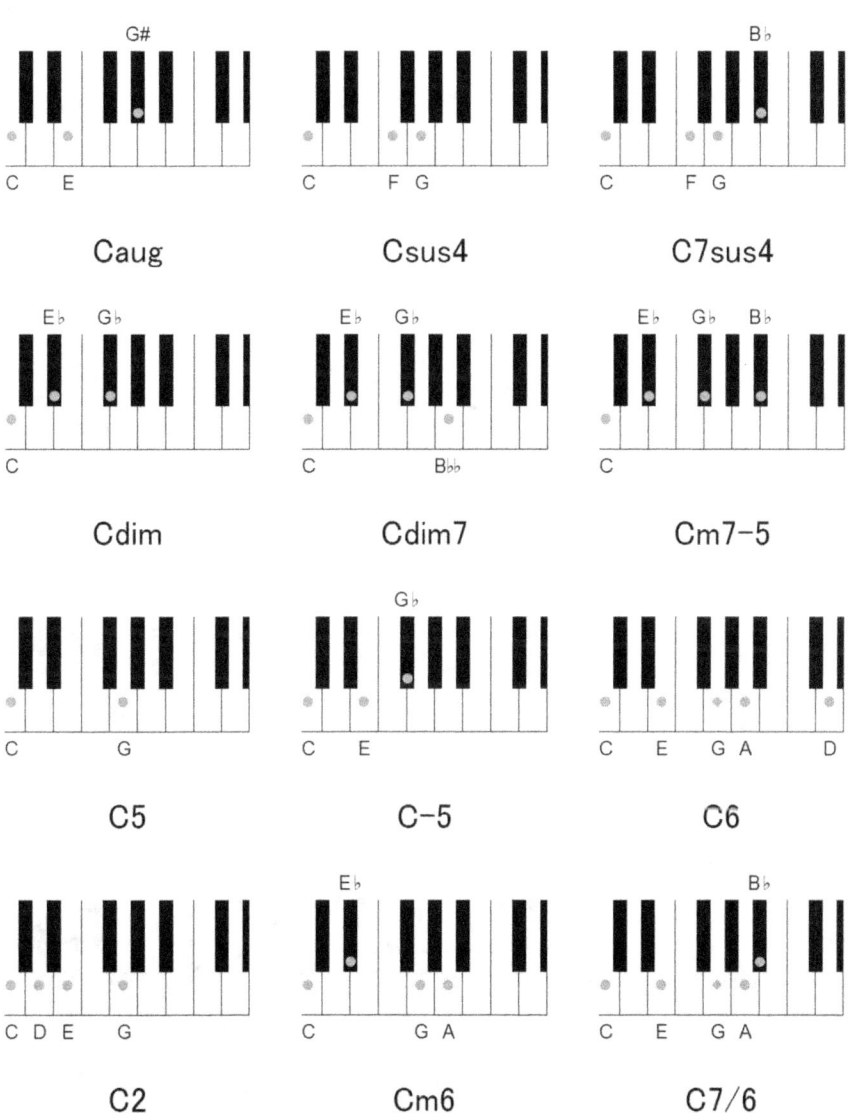

Caug

Csus4

C7sus4

Cdim

Cdim7

Cm7-5

C5

C-5

C6

C2

Cm6

C7/6

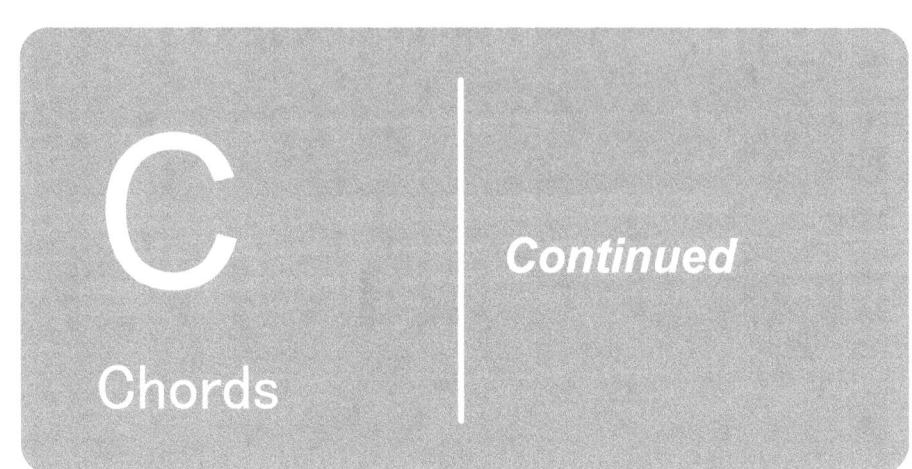

C Chords | Continued

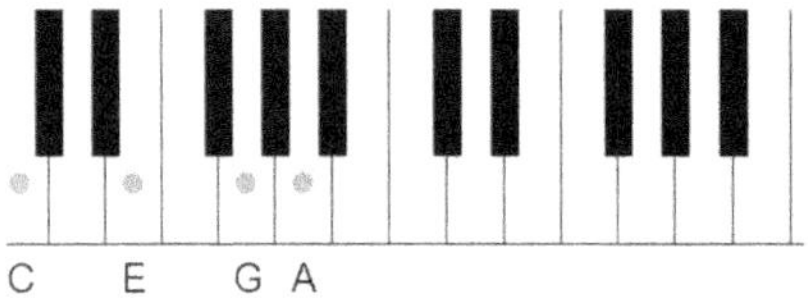

C6/9

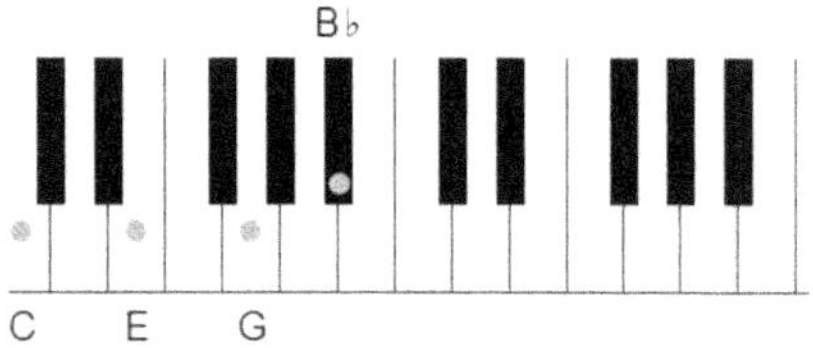

C E G A

Cadd9

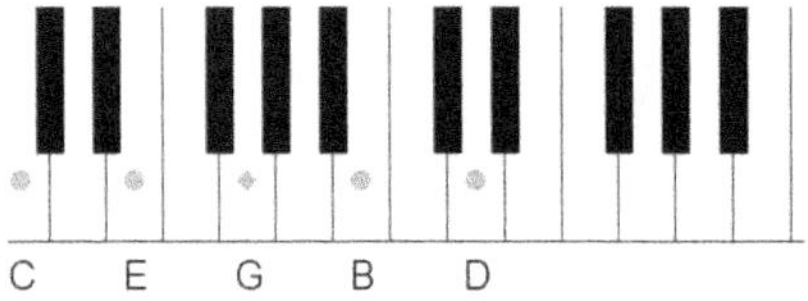

C E G

B♭

Cmaj9

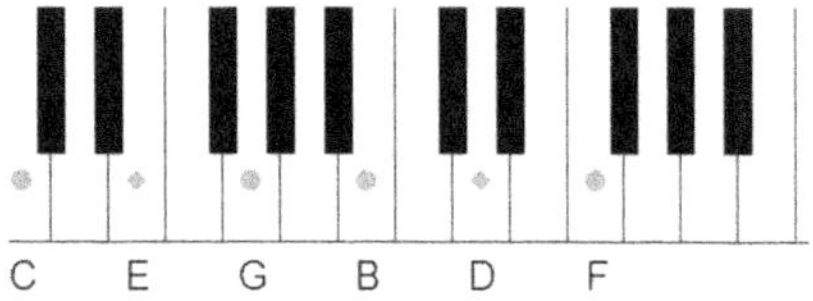

C E G B D

Cmaj11

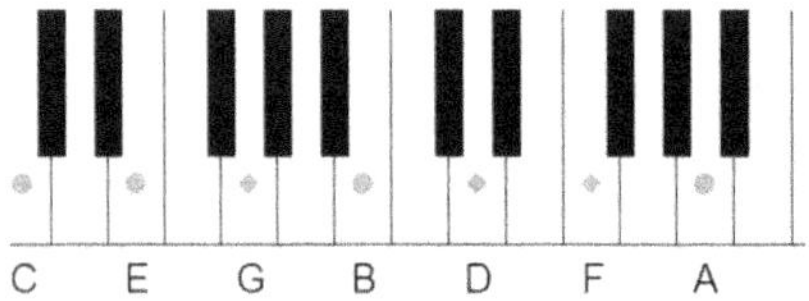

C E G B D F

Cmaj13

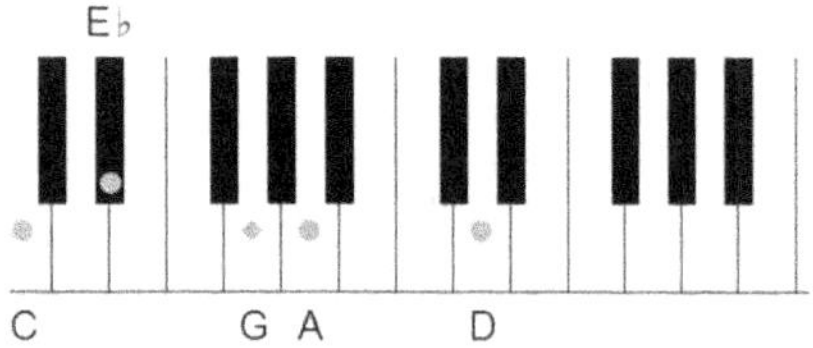

C E G B D F A

Cm6/9

C G A D

E♭

Big Keyboard and Piano Chord Book

©2011 Moran Education http://www.MoranEducation.com/12Notes

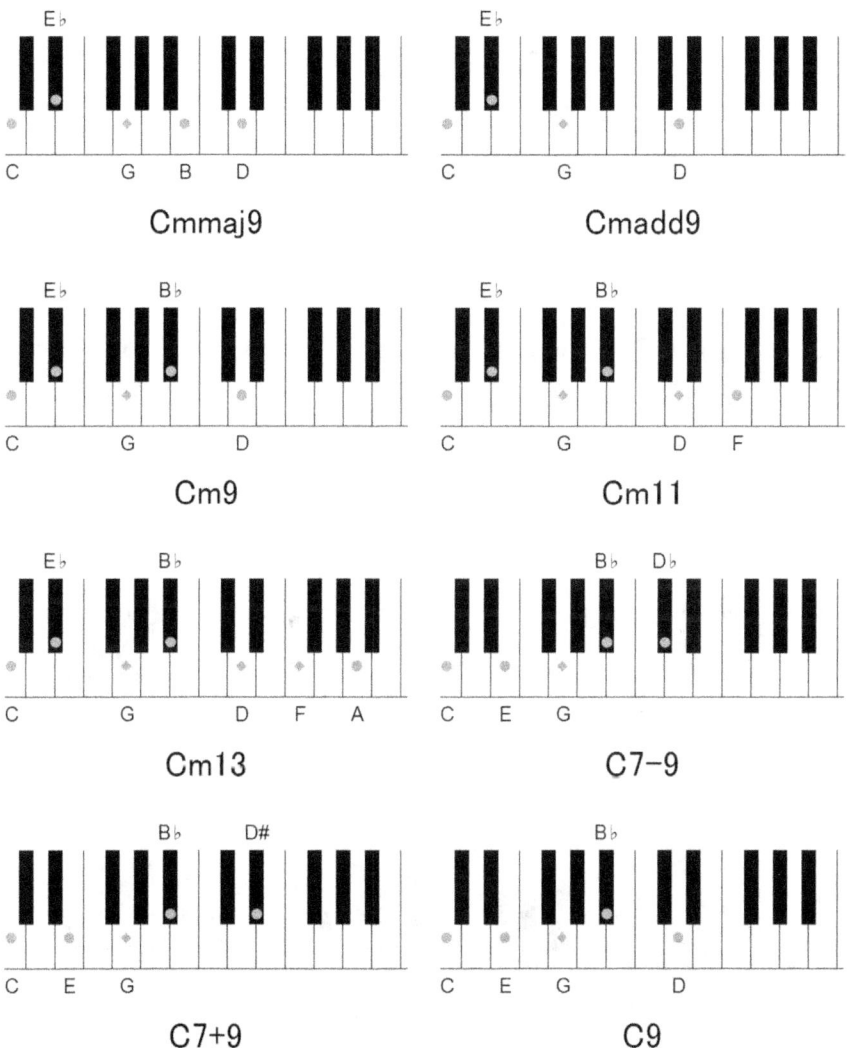

Cmmaj9

Cmadd9

Cm9

Cm11

Cm13

C7-9

C7+9

C9

C Chords

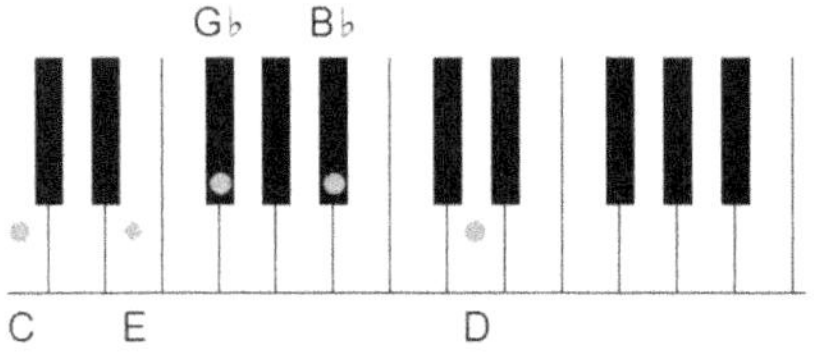

C9-5

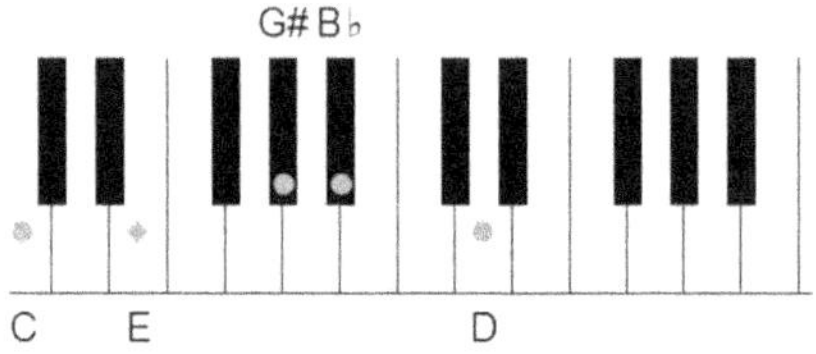

C9+5

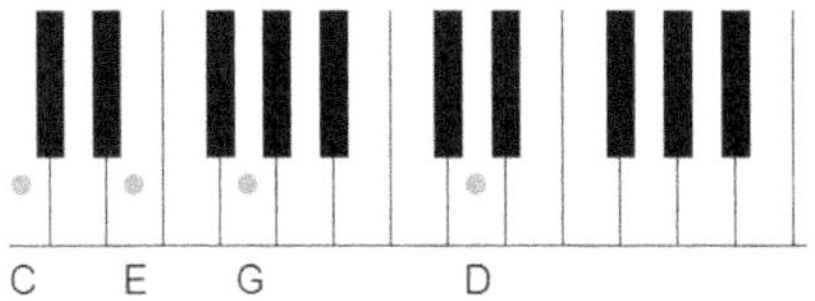

Cadd9

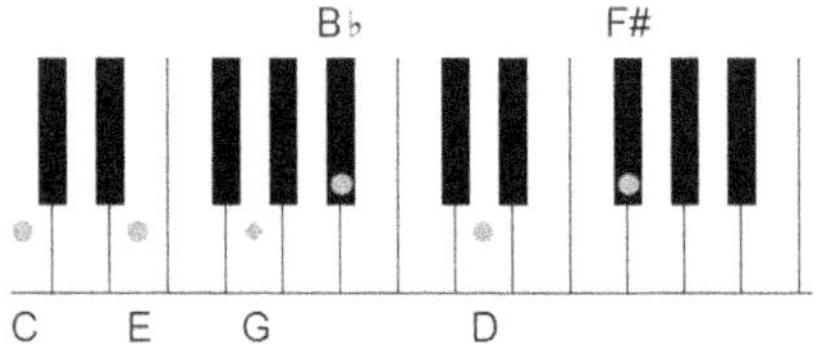

C9+11

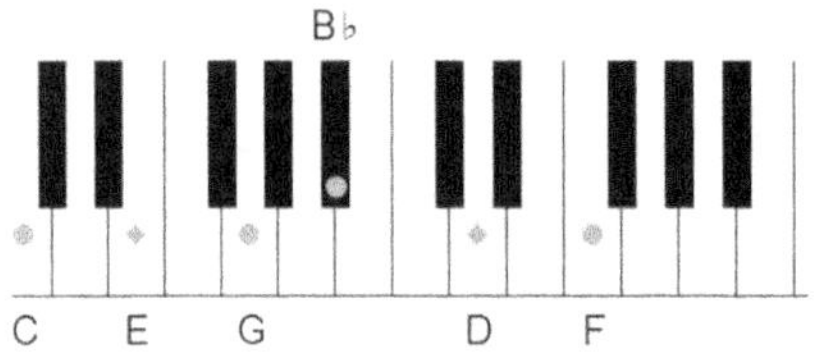

C11

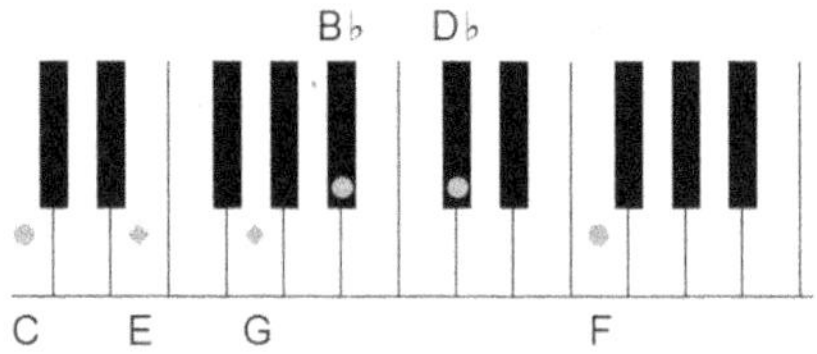

C11-9

Big Keyboard and Piano Chord Book
©2011 Moran Education http://www.MoranEducation.com/12Notes

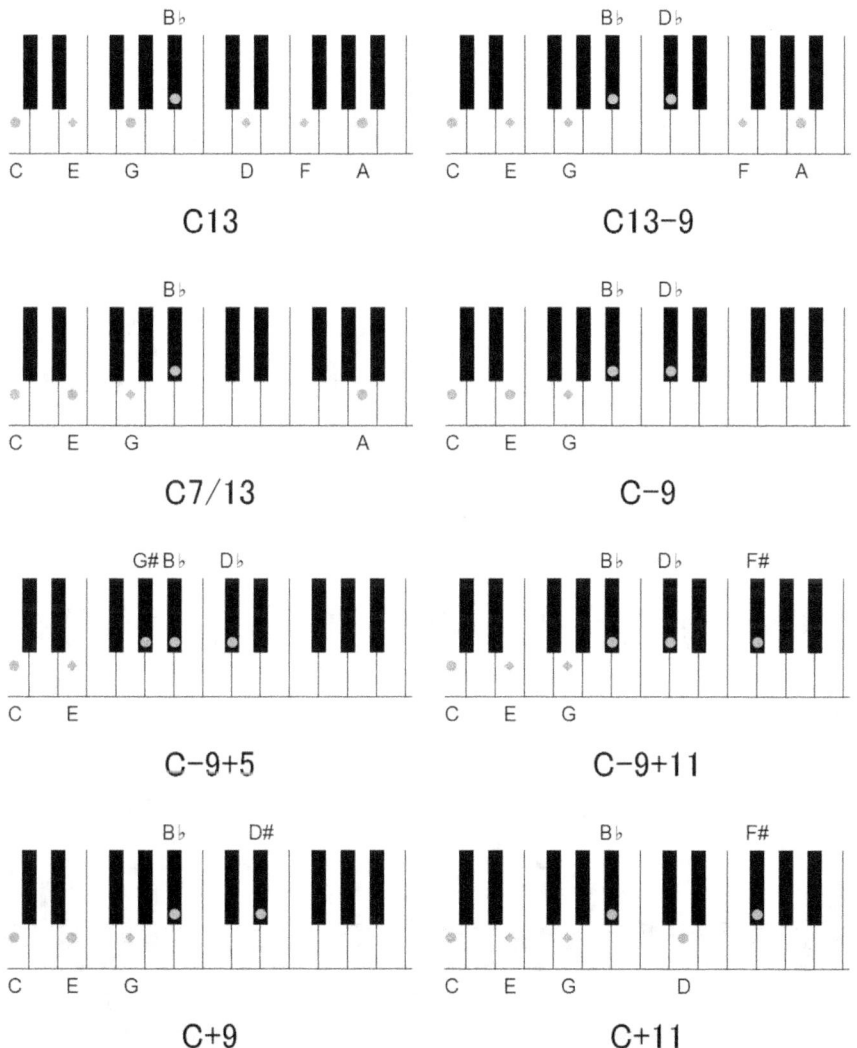

C13

C13-9

C7/13

C-9

C-9+5

C-9+11

C+9

C+11

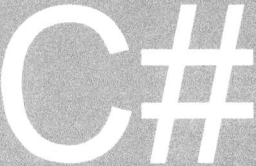

C#

Chords

C# is also known as D♭

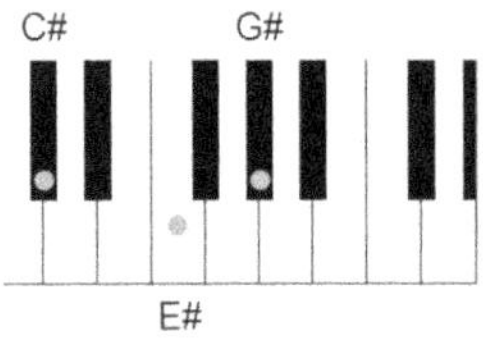

C# Major	C#m	C#7
C#m7	C#maj7	C#mmaj7
C#maj7+5	C#7-5	C#7+5

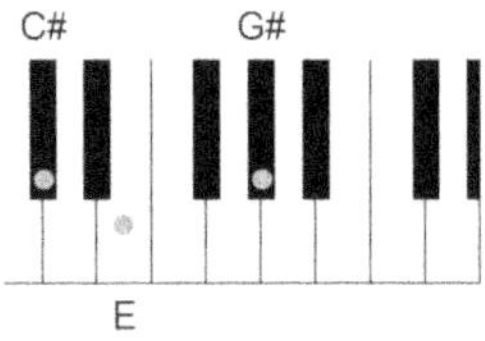

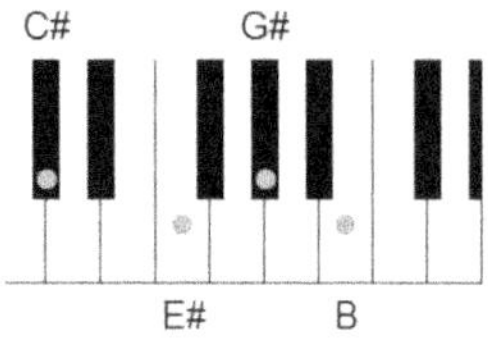

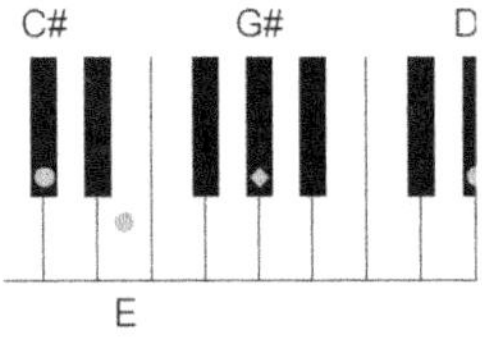

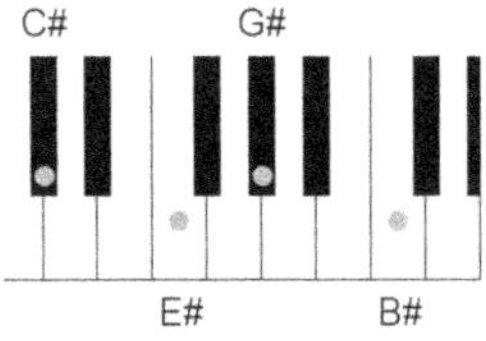

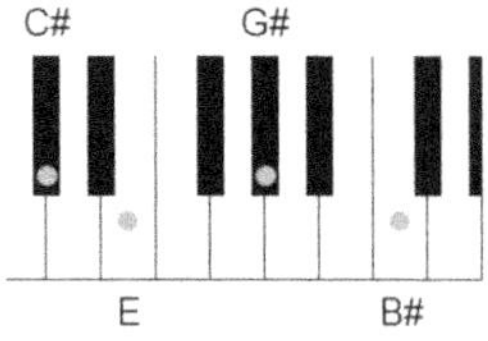

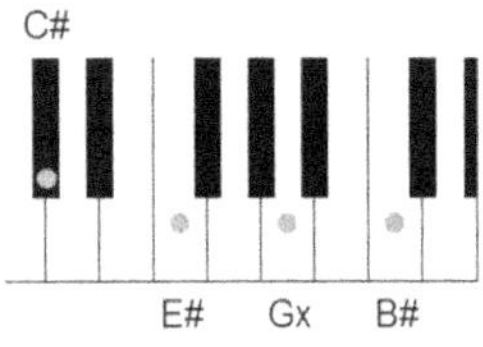

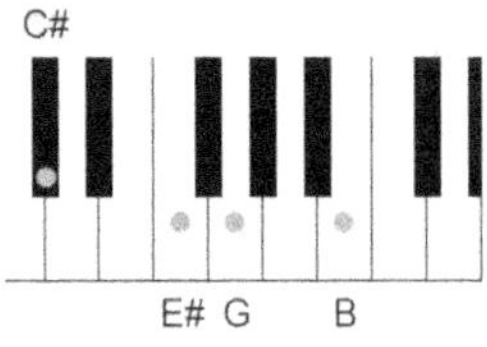

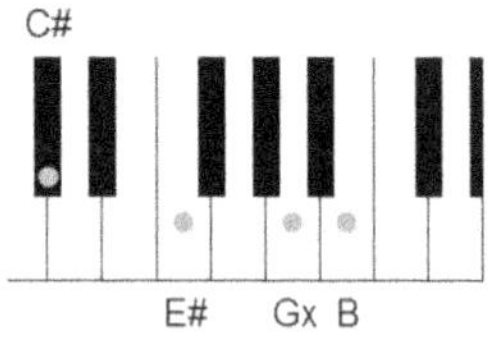

C#

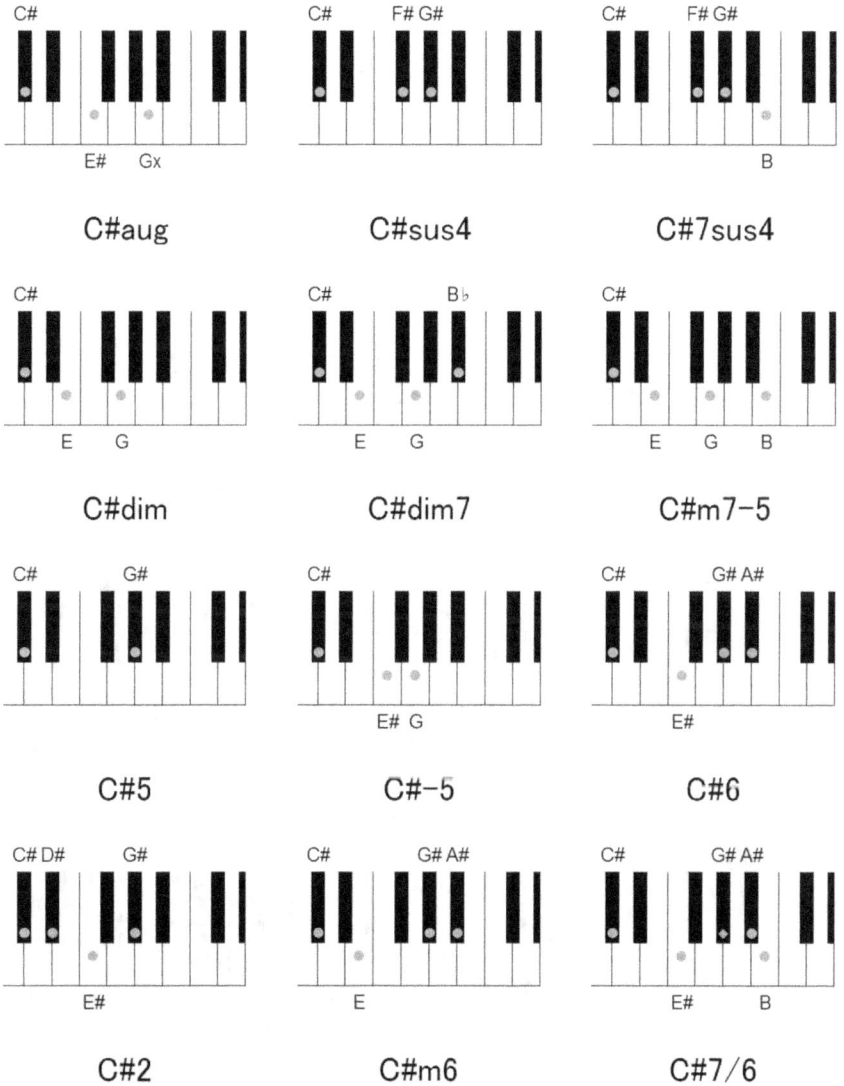

C#aug

C#sus4

C#7sus4

C#dim

C#dim7

C#m7-5

C#5

C#-5

C#6

C#2

C#m6

C#7/6

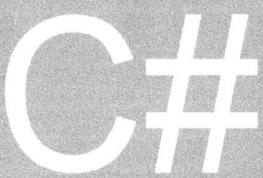

C# Chords | *Continued*

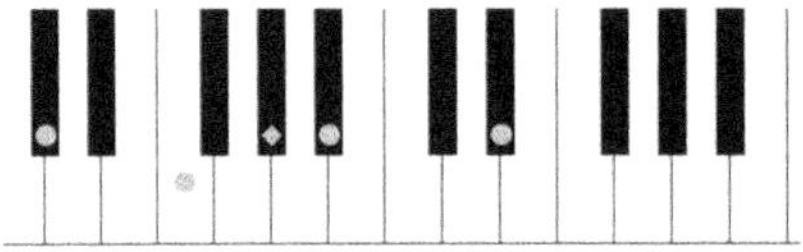

C#   G# A#   D#

E#

C#6/9

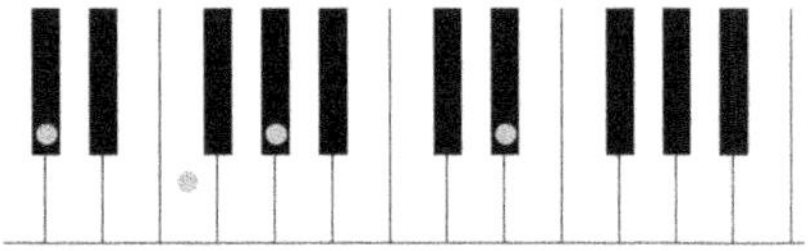

C#   G#   D#

E#

C#add9

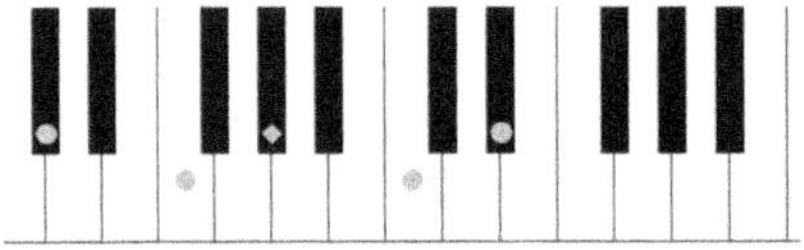

C#   G#   D#

E#   B#

C#maj9

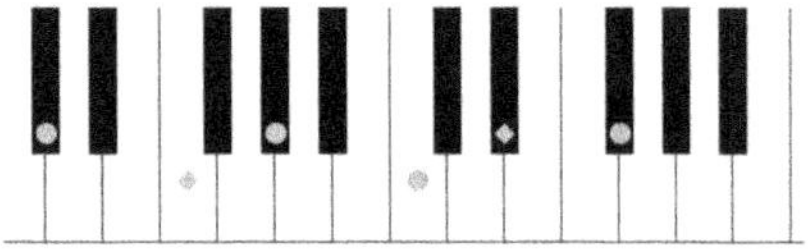

C#   G#   D#   F#

E#   B#

C#maj11

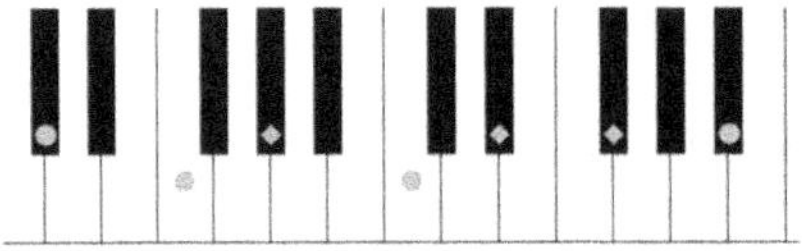

C#   G#   D#   F#   A#

E#   B#

C#maj13

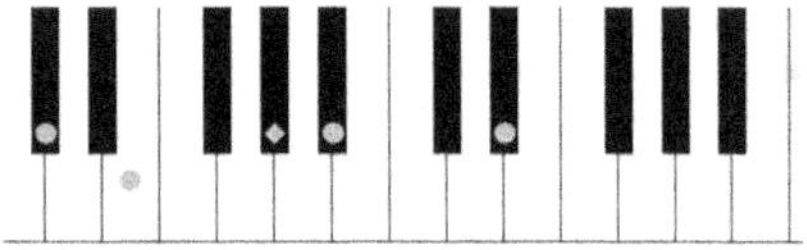

C#   G# A#   D#

E

C#m6/9

Big Keyboard and Piano Chord Book

©2011 Moran Education http://www.MoranEducation.com/12Notes

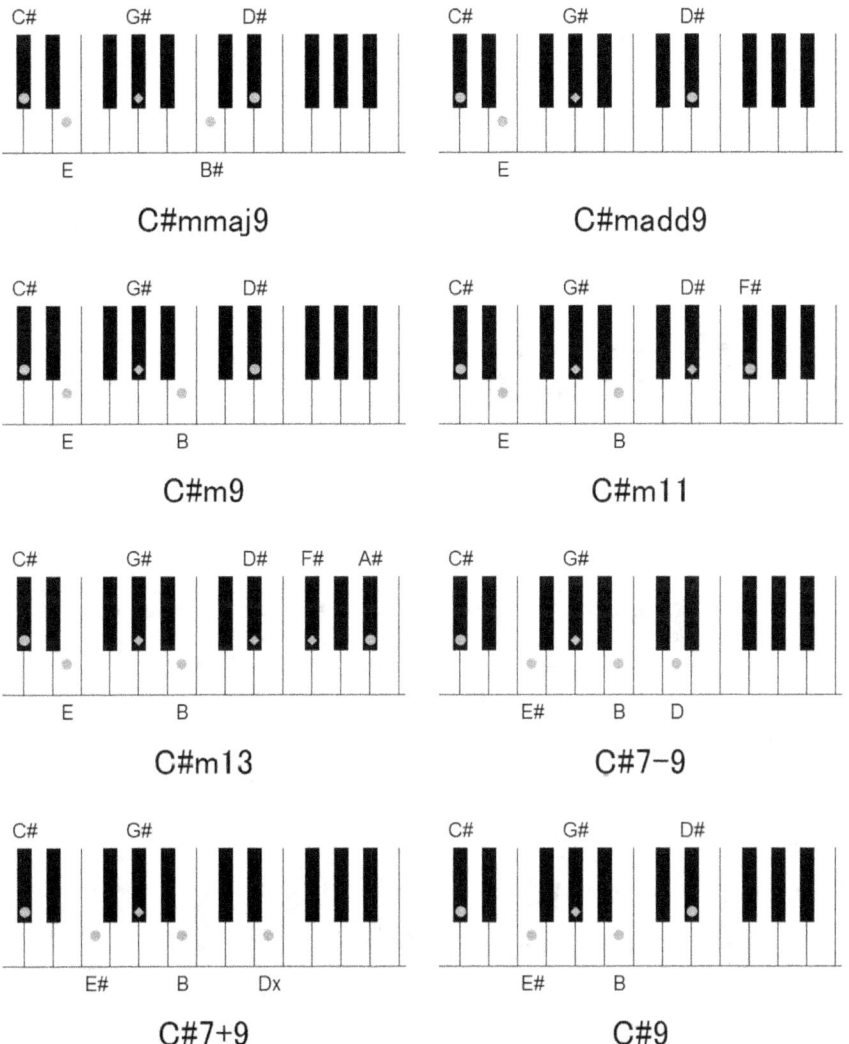

C#mmaj9

C#madd9

C#m9

C#m11

C#m13

C#7-9

C#7+9

C#9

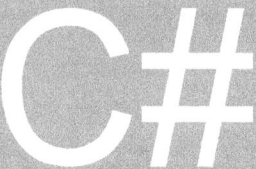

C# | *Continued*
Chords

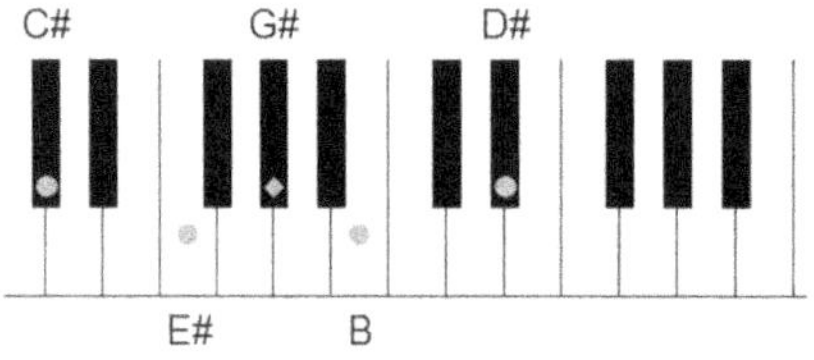

C#9-5

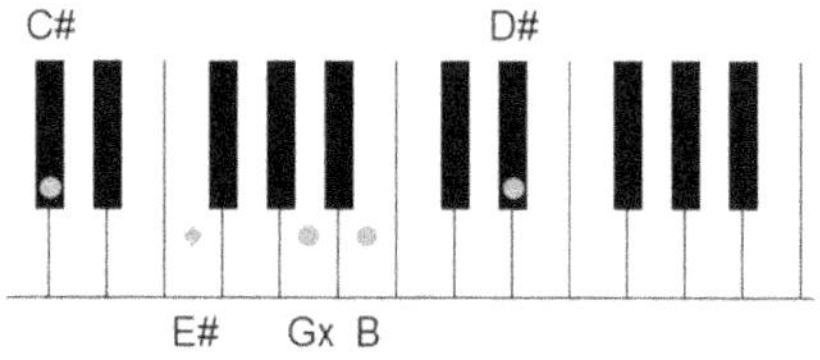

C#9+5

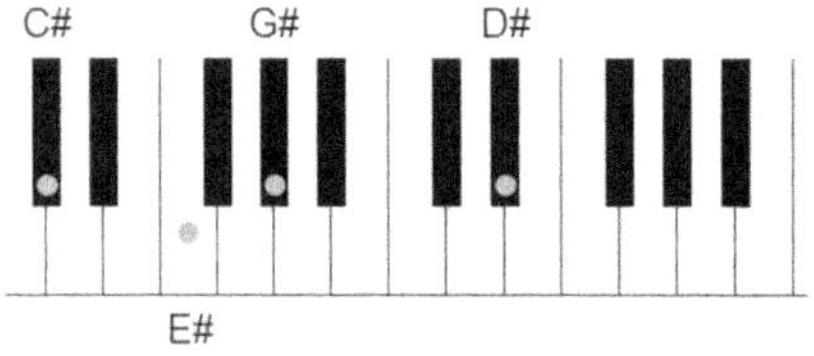

C#add9

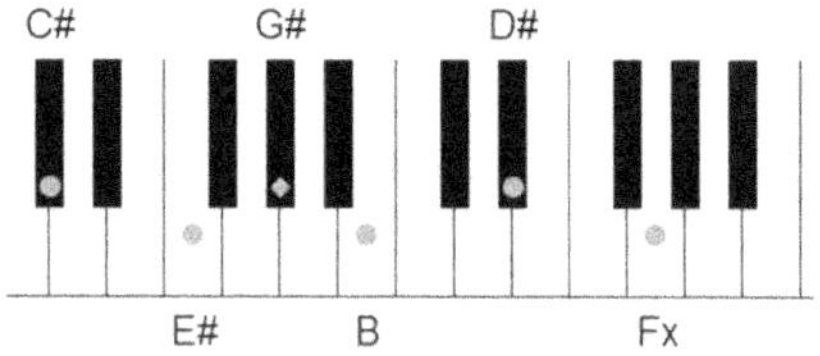

C#9+11

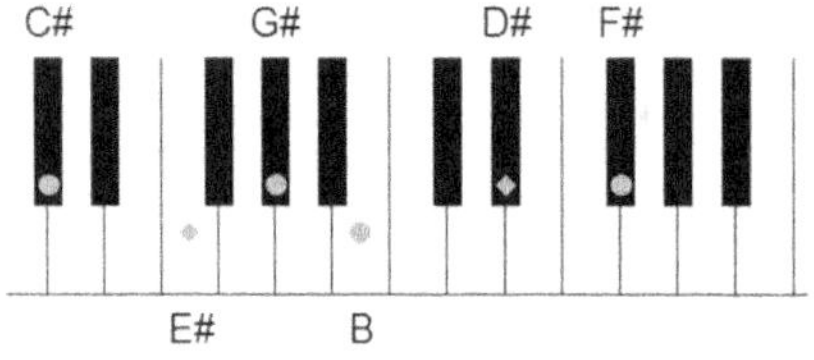

C#11

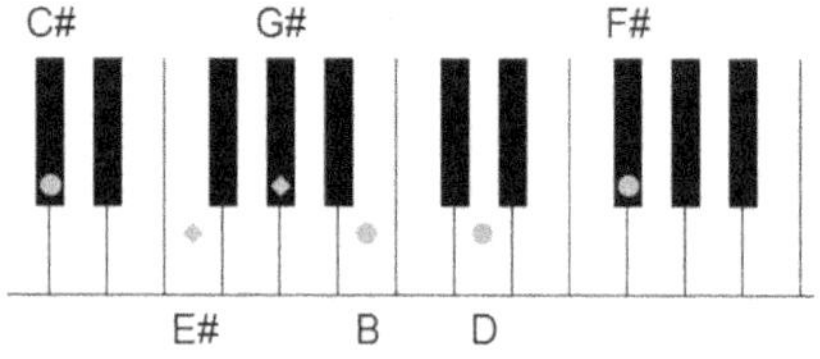

C#11-9

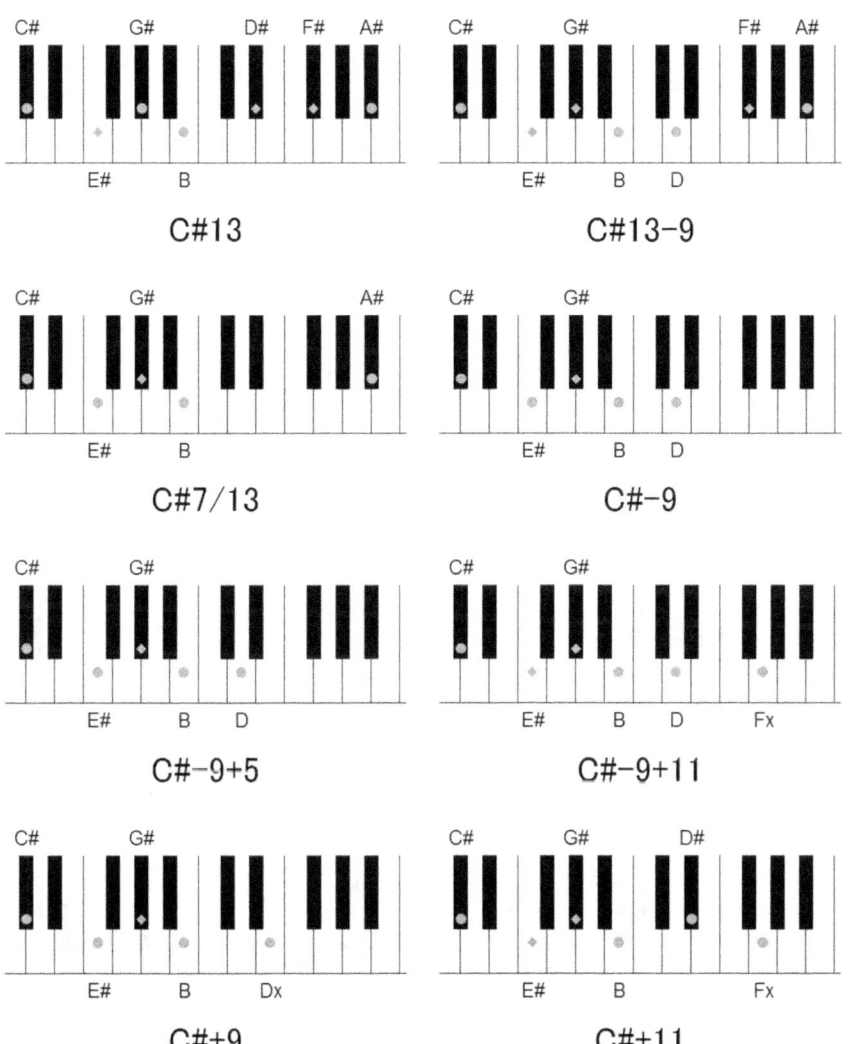

C#13

C#13-9

C#7/13

C#-9

C#-9+5

C#-9+11

C#+9

C#+11

D

Chords

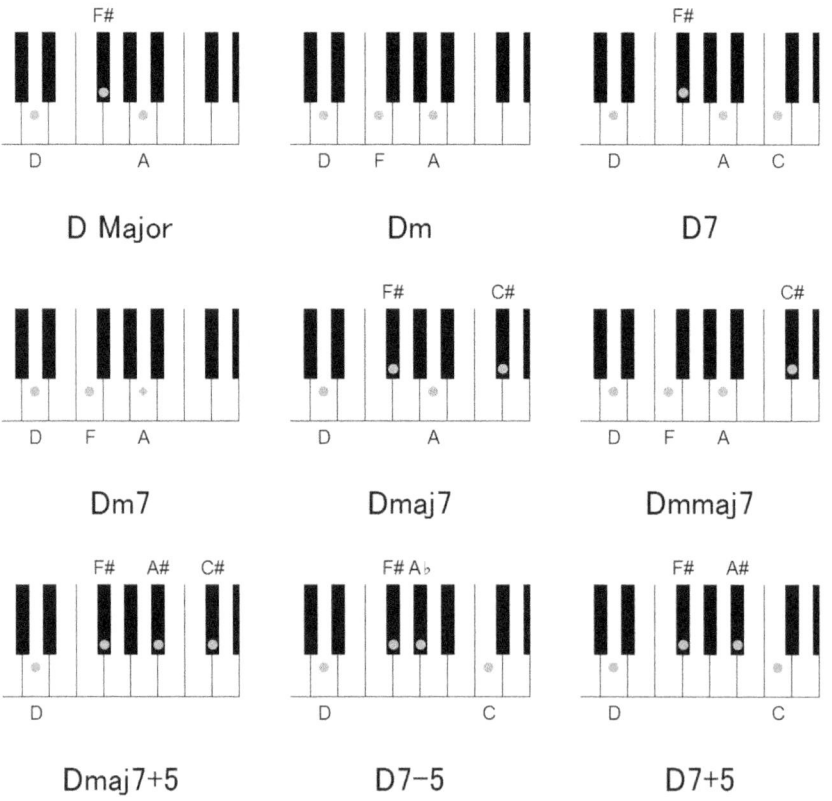

F#

D A

D Major

D F A

Dm

F#

D A C

D7

D F A

Dm7

F# C#

D A

Dmaj7

C#

D F A

Dmmaj7

F# A# C#

D

Dmaj7+5

F# A♭

D C

D7−5

F# A#

D C

D7+5

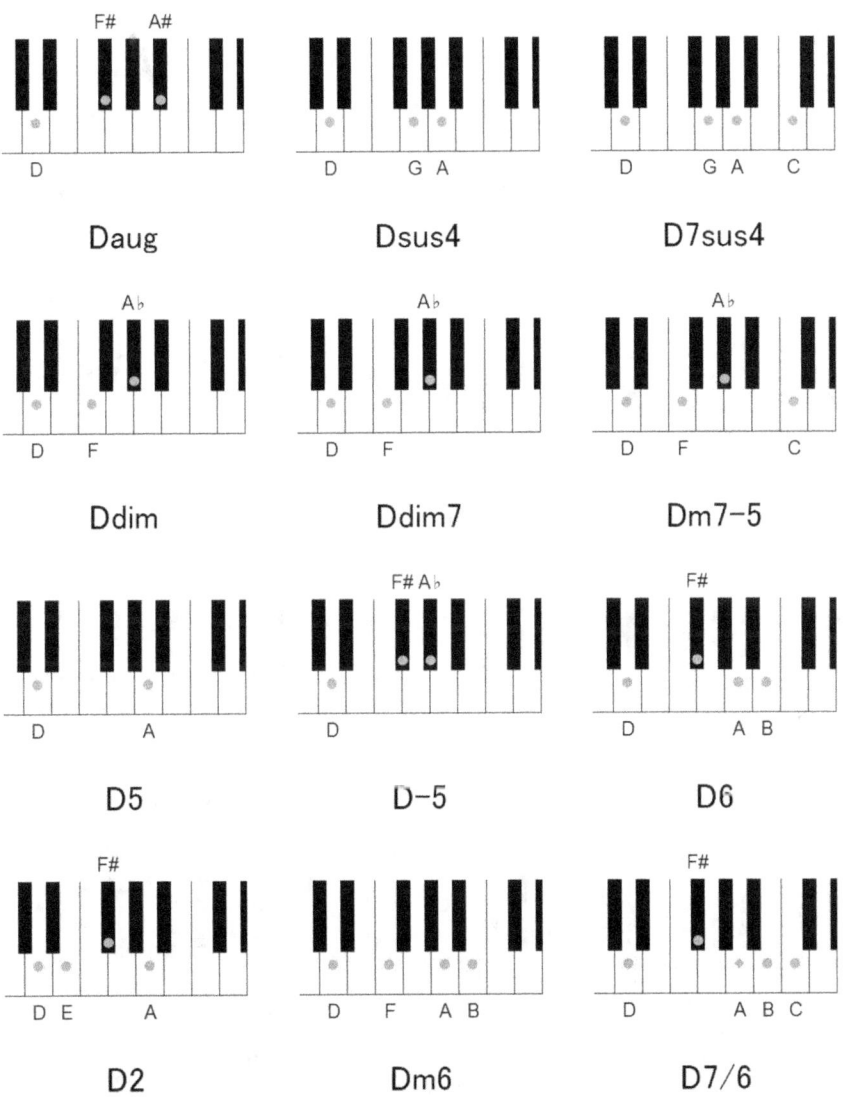

Daug

Dsus4

D7sus4

Ddim

Ddim7

Dm7-5

D5

D-5

D6

D2

Dm6

D7/6

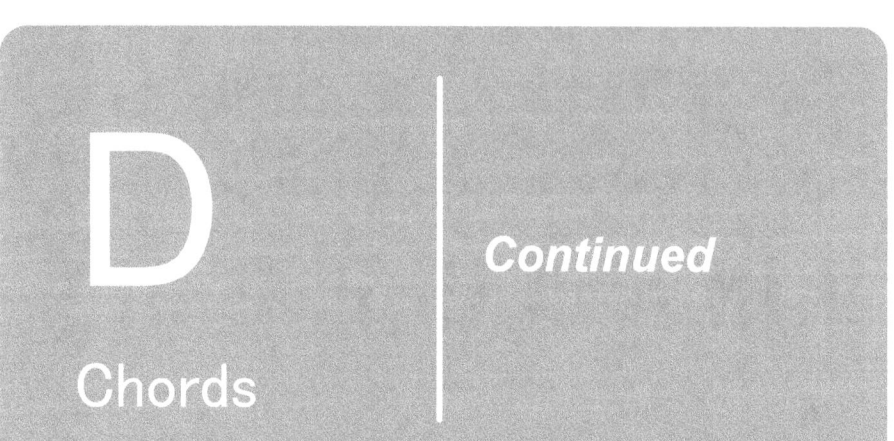

D
Chords

Continued

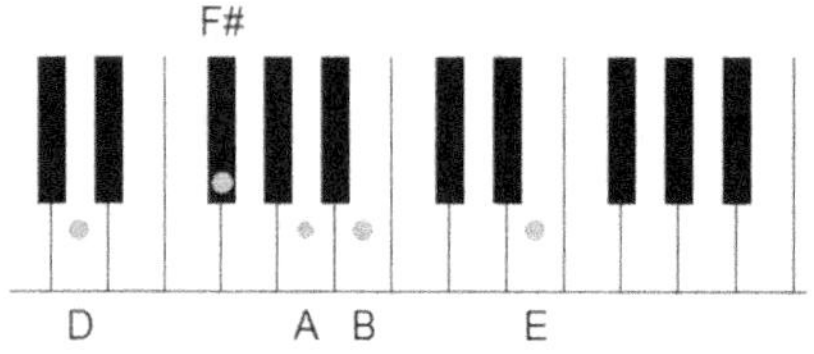

D6/9

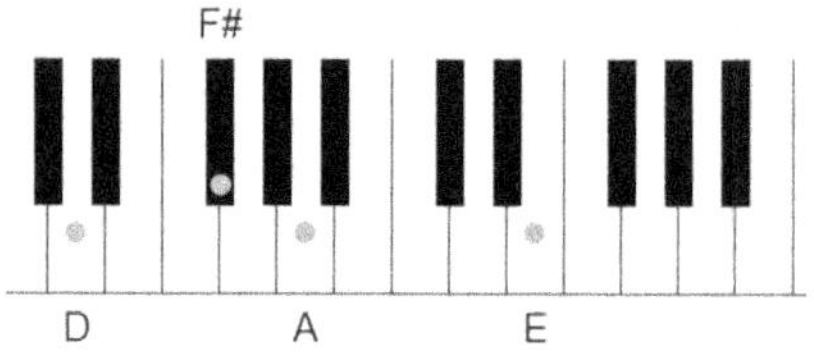

F#

D   A B   E

Dadd9

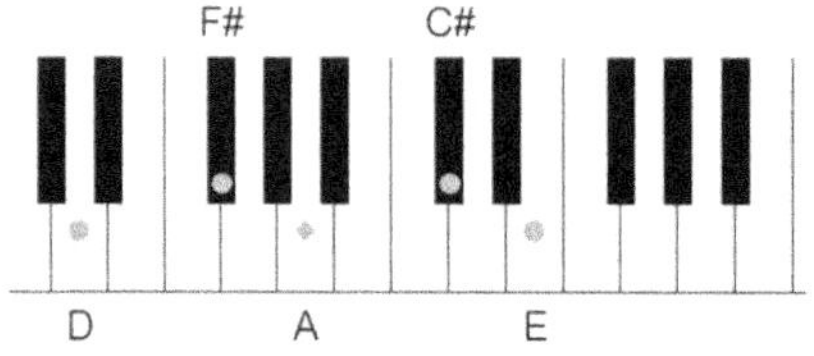

F#

D   A   E

Dmaj9

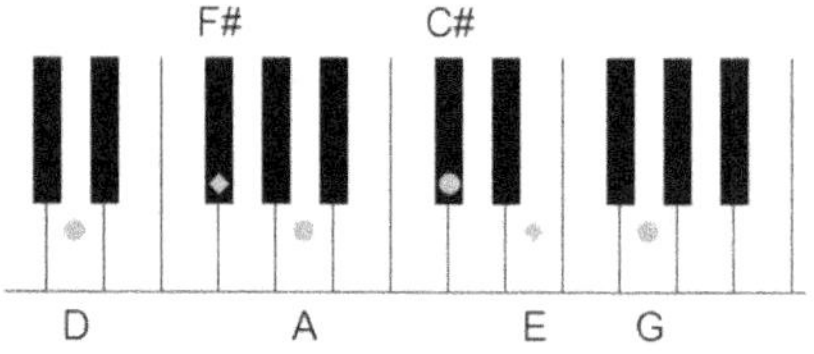

F#   C#

D   A   E

Dmaj11

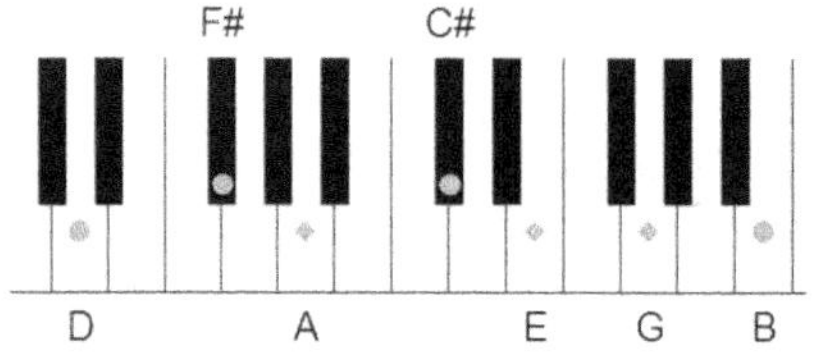

F#   C#

D   A   E   G

Dmaj13

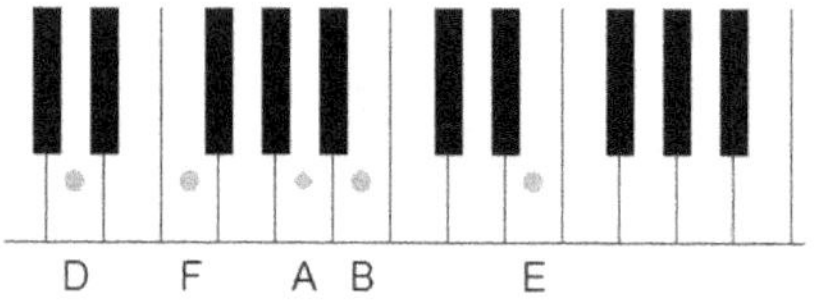

F#   C#

D   A   E   G   B

Dm6/9

D   F   A B   E

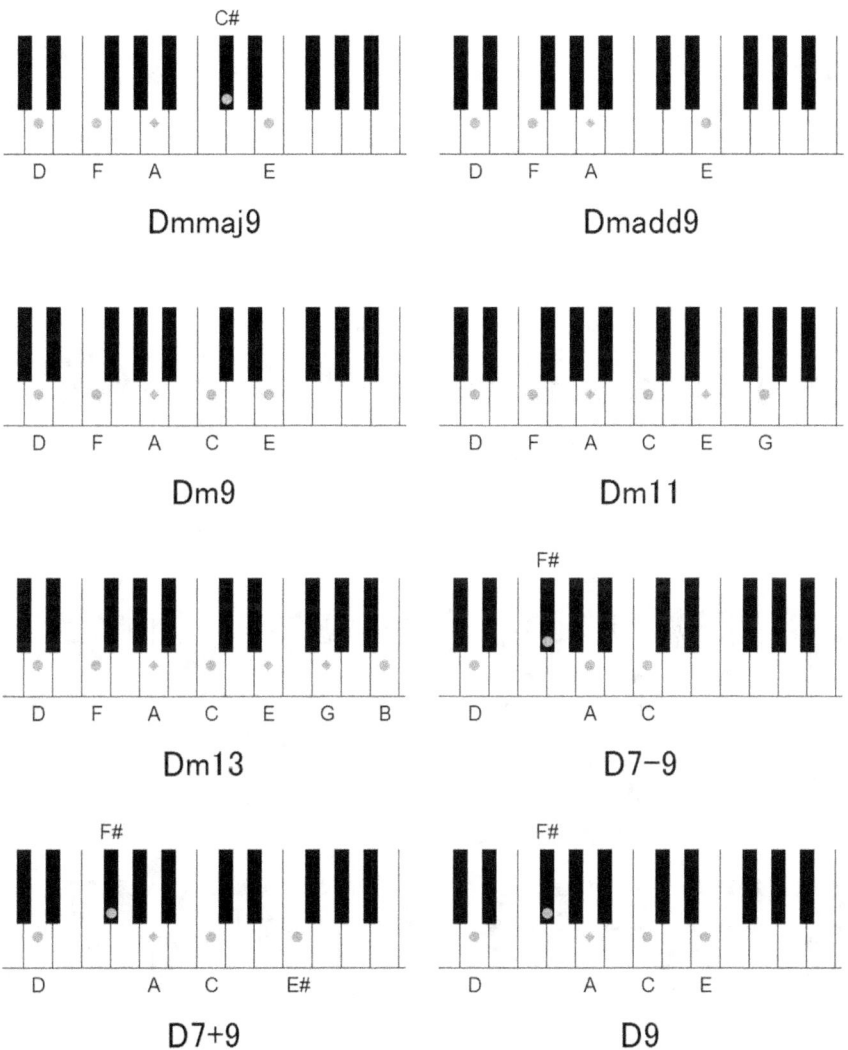

D

Chords

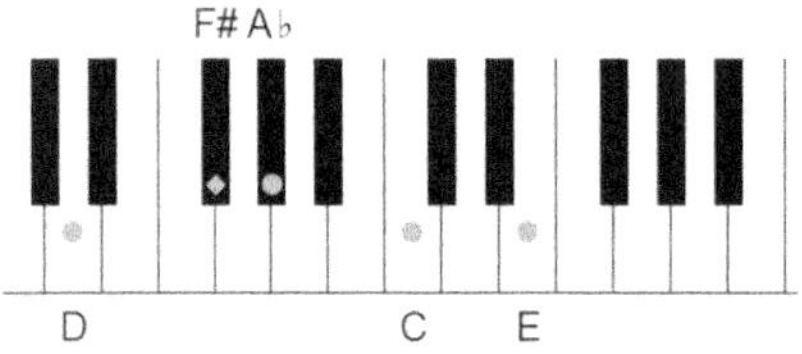

D9−5

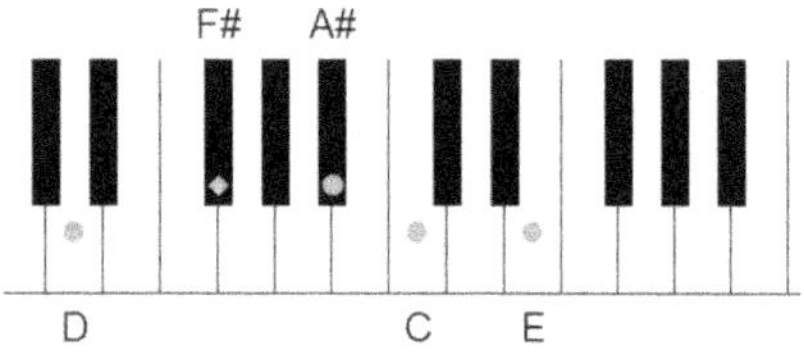

F# Ab

D   C   E

D9+5

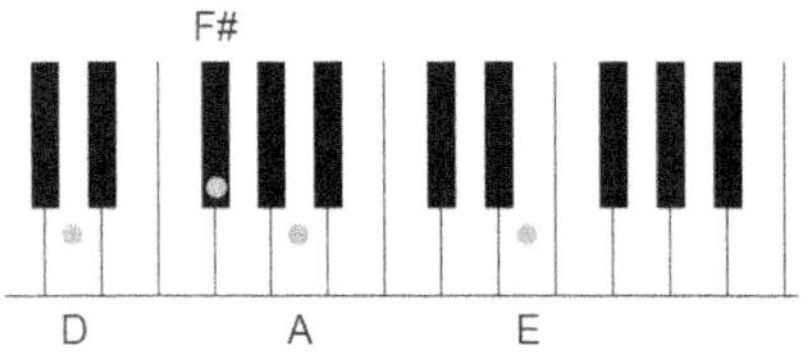

F#   A#

D   C   E

Dadd9

F#

D   A   E

D9+11

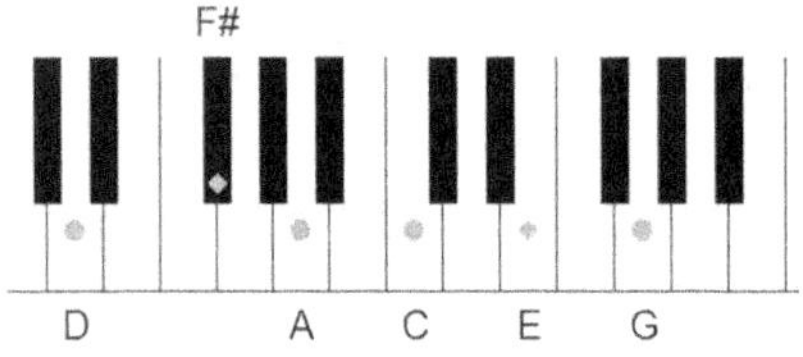

F#   G#

D   A   C   E

D11

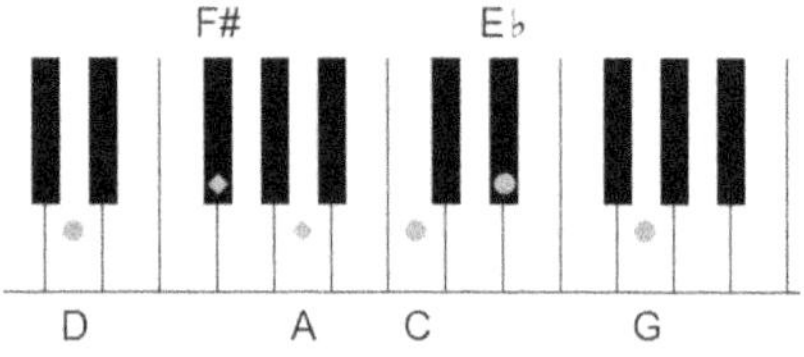

F#

D   A   C   E   G

D11−9

F#   Eb

D   A   C   G

Big Keyboard and Piano Chord Book
©2011 Moran Education http://www.MoranEducation.com/12Notes

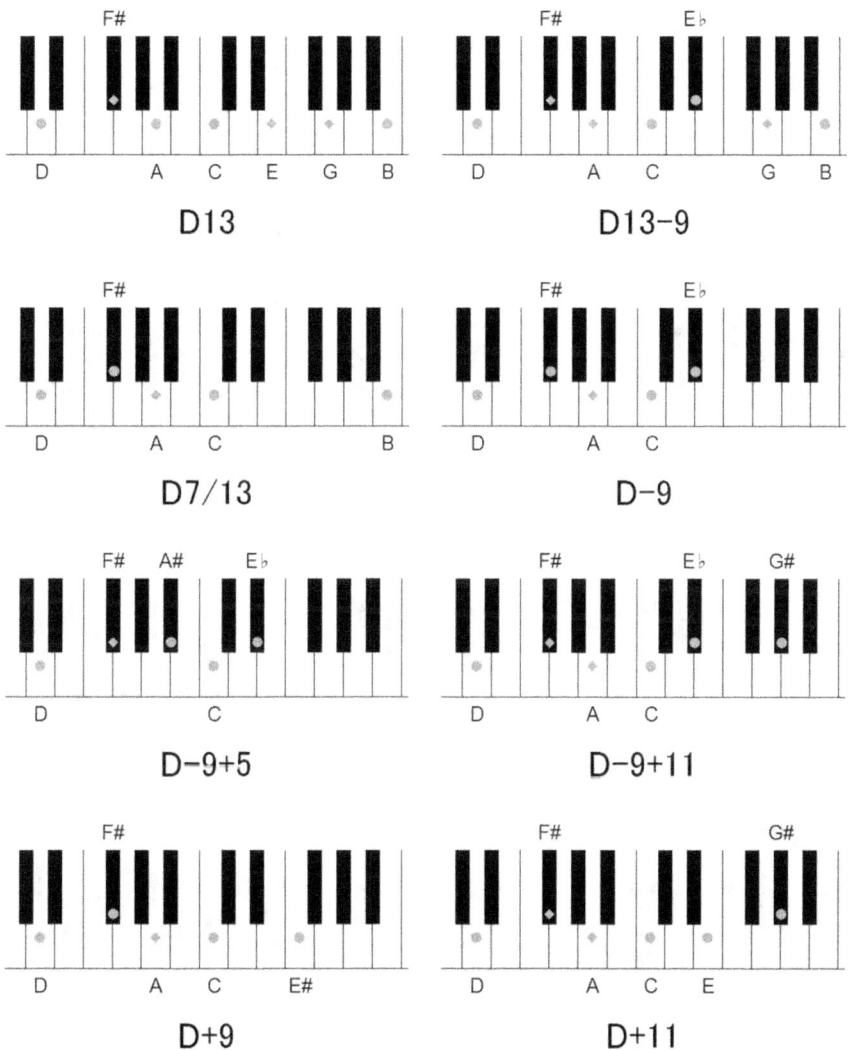

D13

D13-9

D7/13

D-9

D-9+5

D-9+11

D+9

D+11

E♭ Chords

E♭ is also known as D#

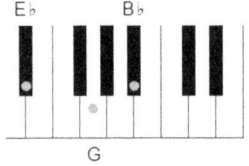

E♭ Major

E♭ m

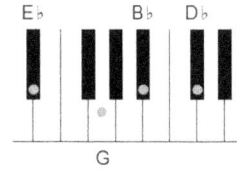

E♭ 7

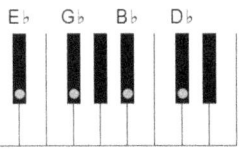

E♭ m7

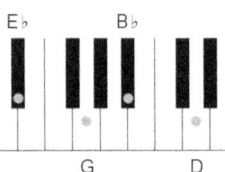

E♭ maj7

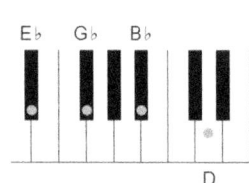

E♭ mmaj7

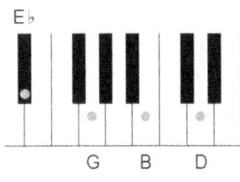

E♭ maj7+5

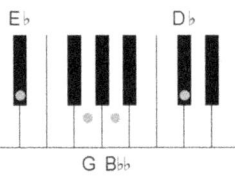

E♭ 7−5

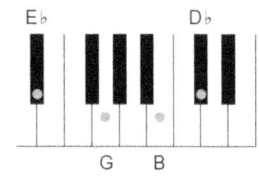

E♭ 7+5

E♭

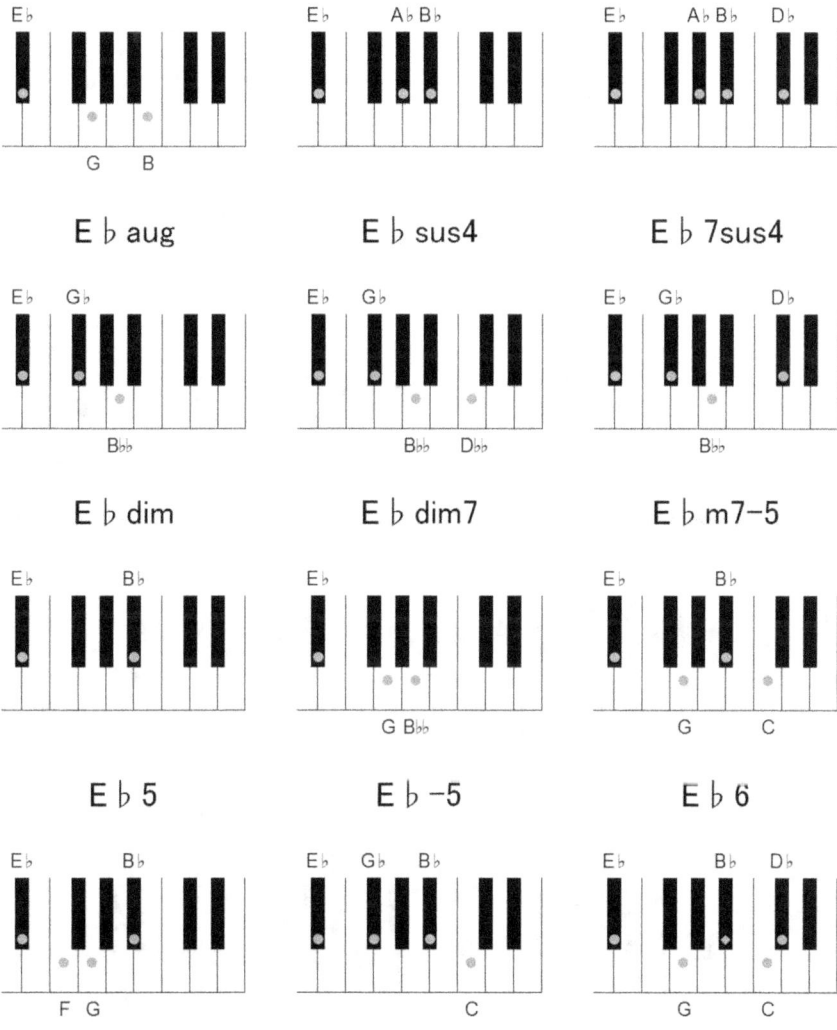

E♭ aug

E♭ sus4

E♭ 7sus4

E♭ dim

E♭ dim7

E♭ m7-5

E♭ 5

E♭ -5

E♭ 6

E♭ 2

E♭ m6

E♭ 7/6

E♭ Chords
Continued

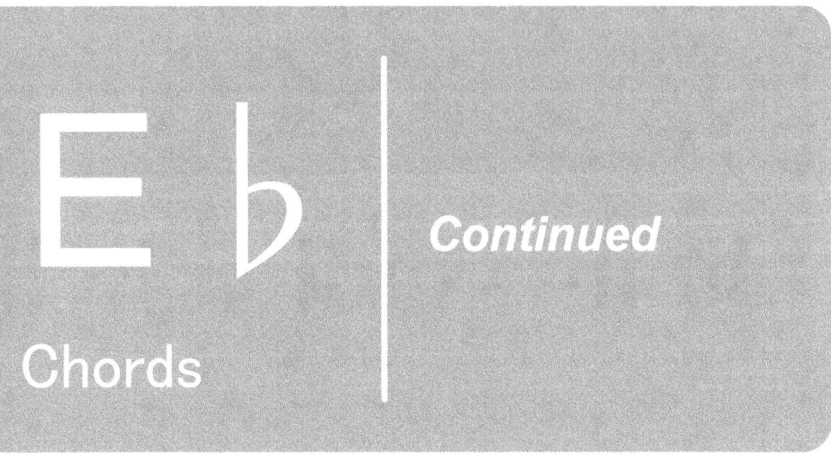

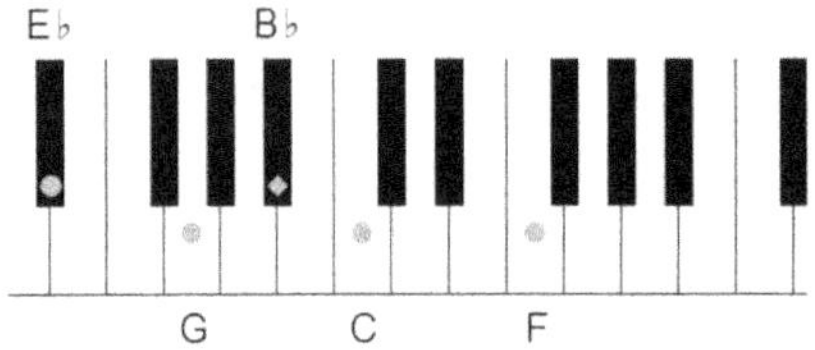

E♭ 6/9

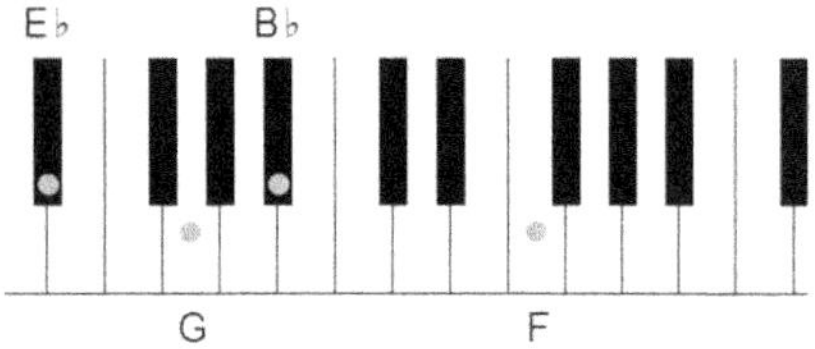

E♭ add9

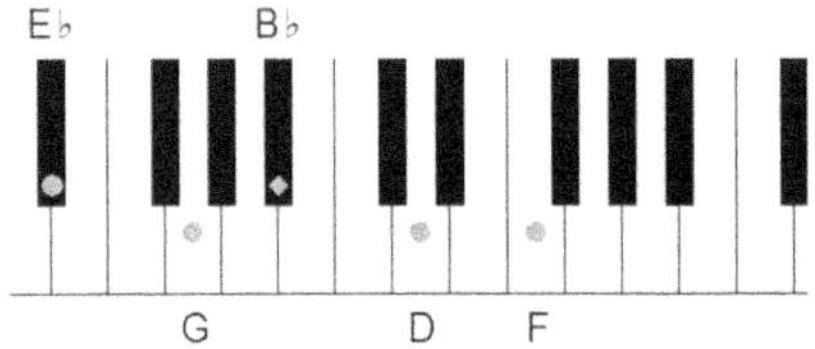

E♭ maj9

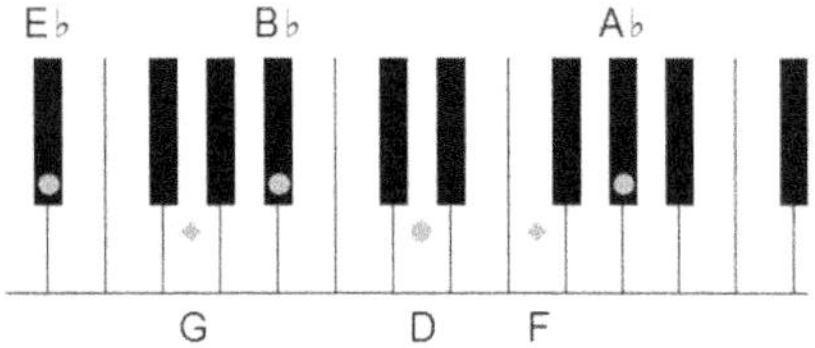

E♭ maj11

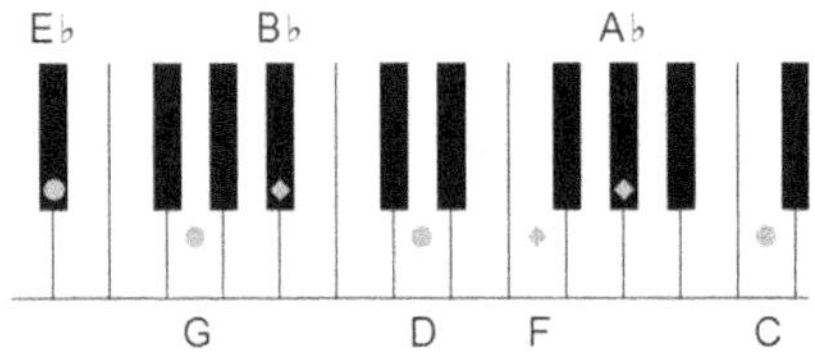

E♭ maj13

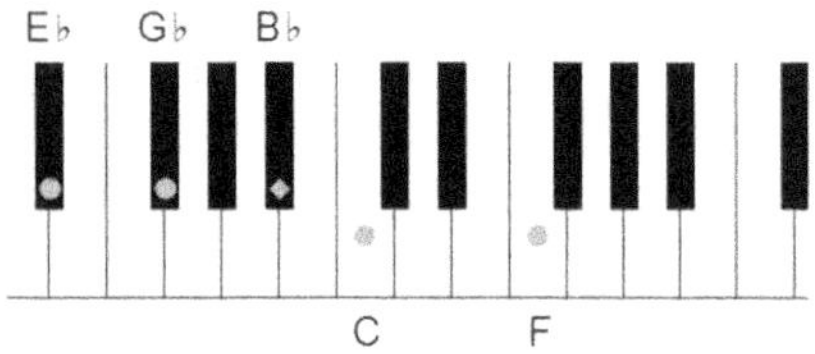

E♭ m6/9

E♭

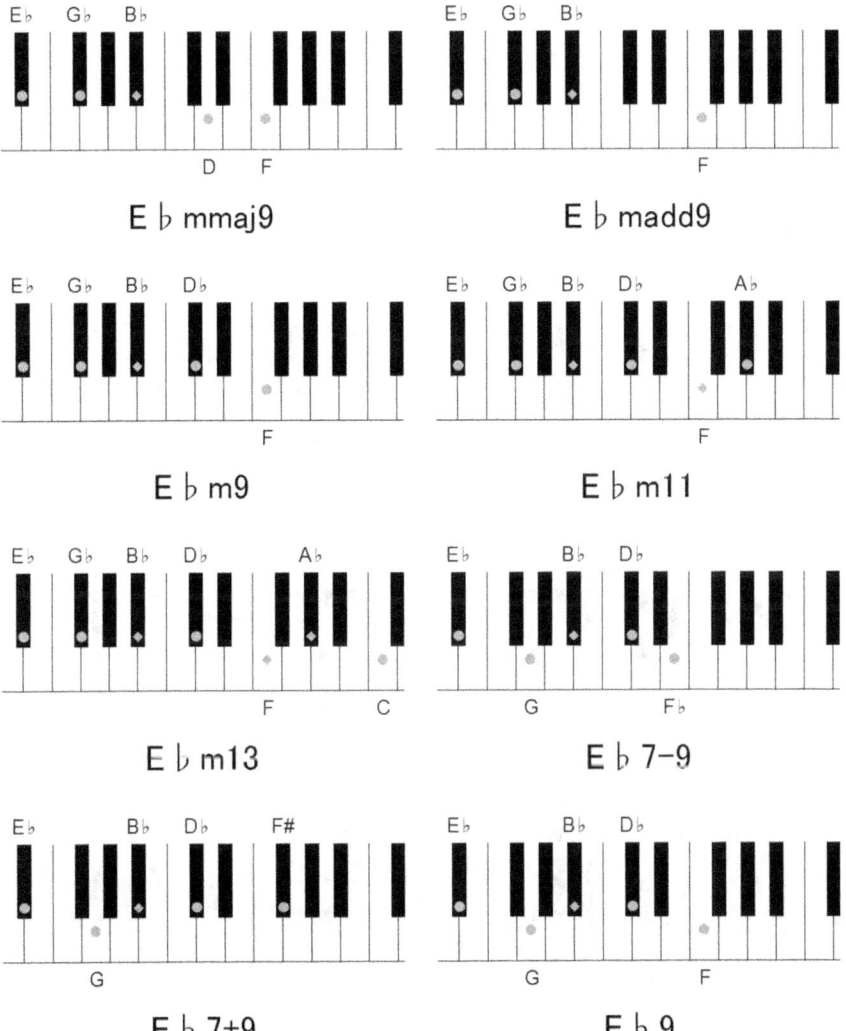

E♭ mmaj9

E♭ madd9

E♭ m9

E♭ m11

E♭ m13

E♭ 7-9

E♭ 7+9

E♭ 9

Chords

Continued

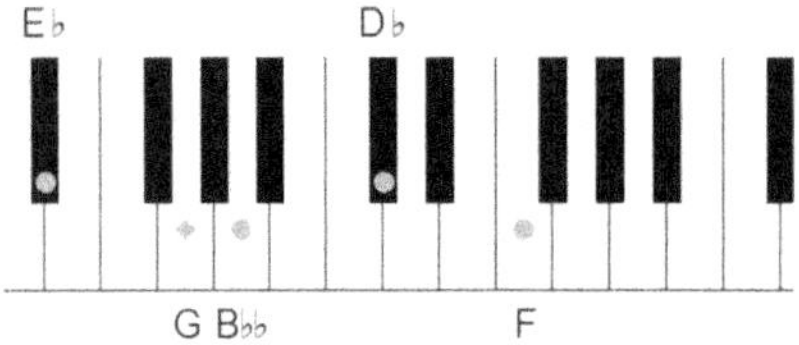

E♭ 9-5	E♭ 9+5
E♭ add9	E♭ 9+11
E♭ 11	E♭ 11-9

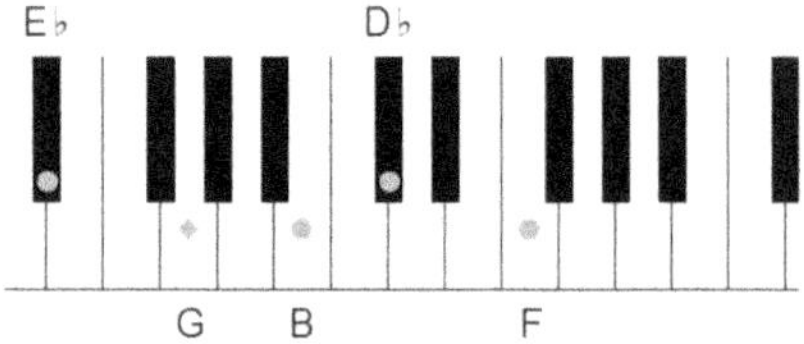

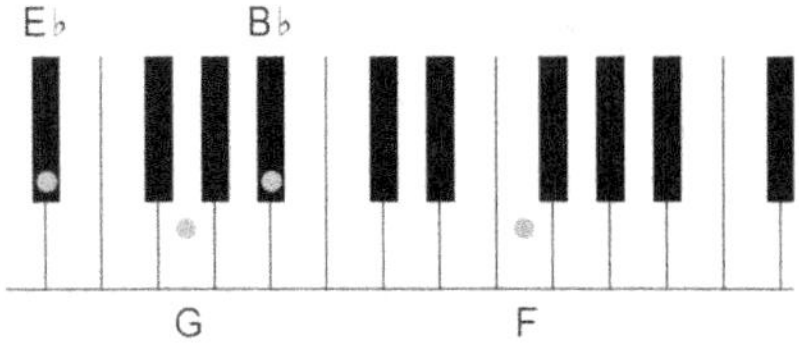

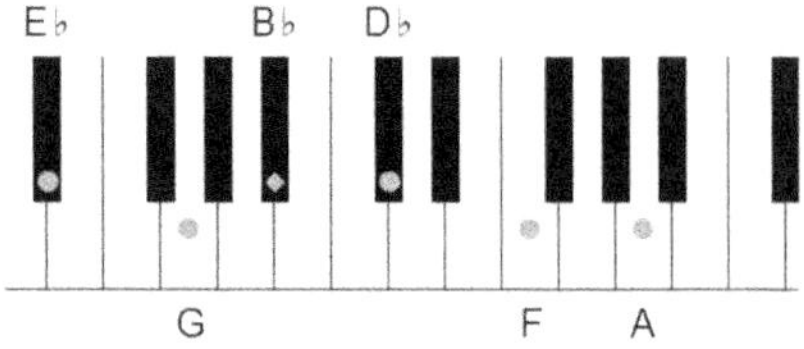

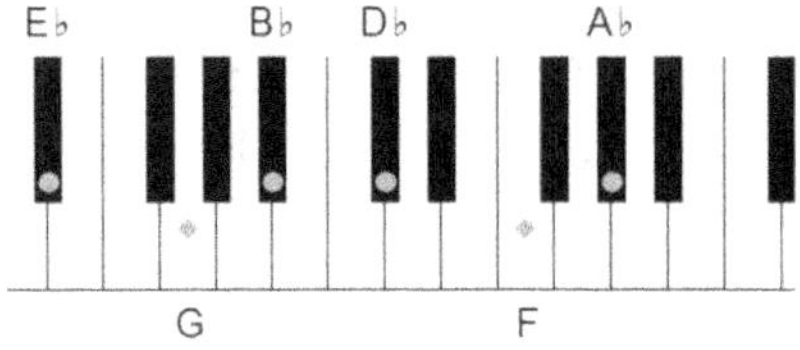

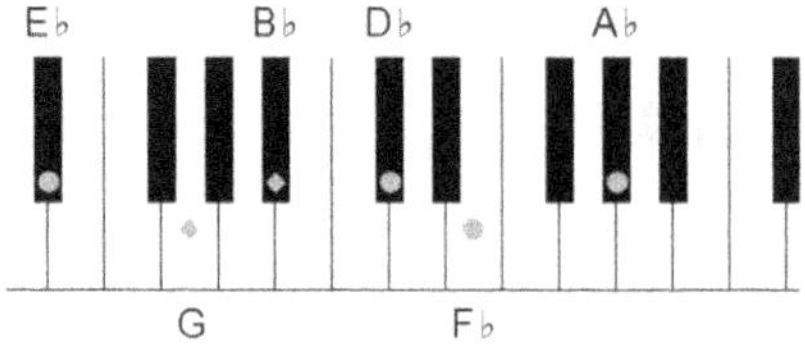

Big Keyboard and Piano Chord Book
©2011 Moran Education http://www.MoranEducation.com/12Notes

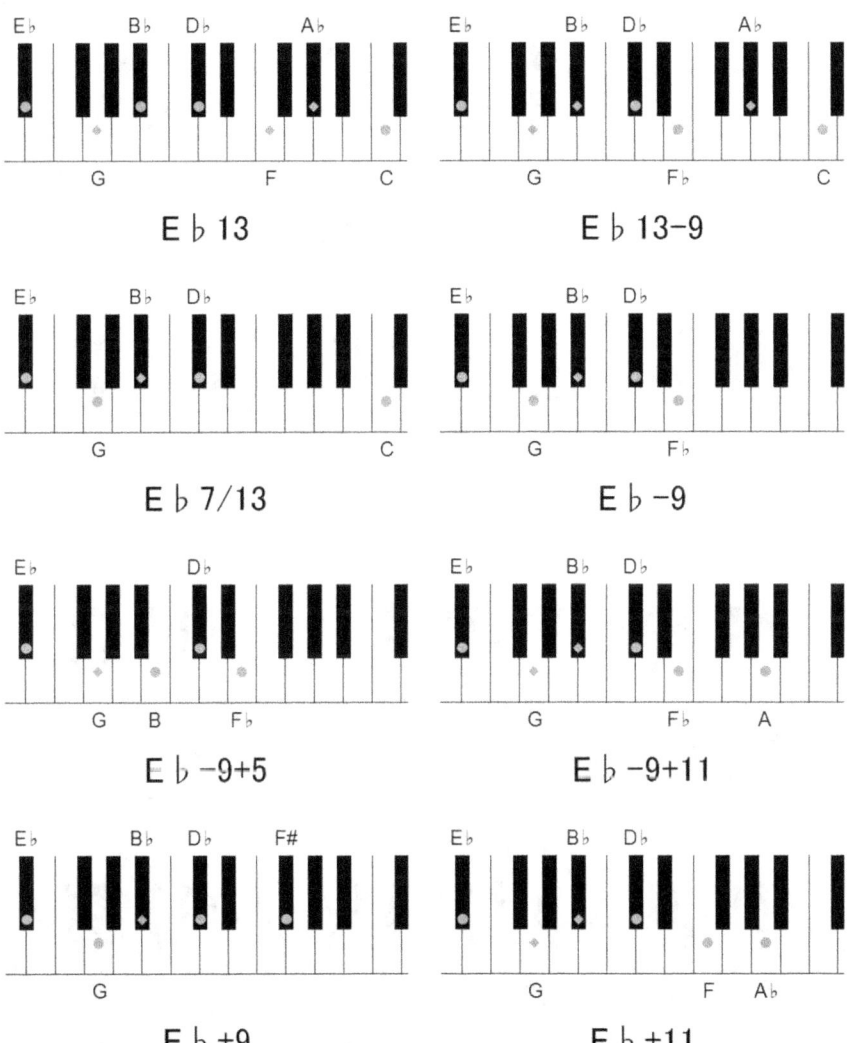

E♭ 13

E♭ 13-9

E♭ 7/13

E♭ -9

E♭ -9+5

E♭ -9+11

E♭ +9

E♭ +11

E

Chords

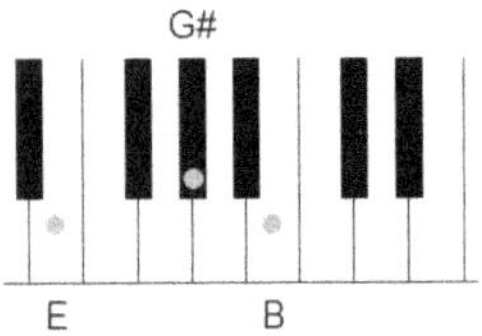

E Major

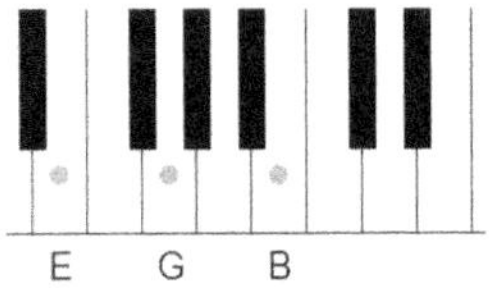

Em

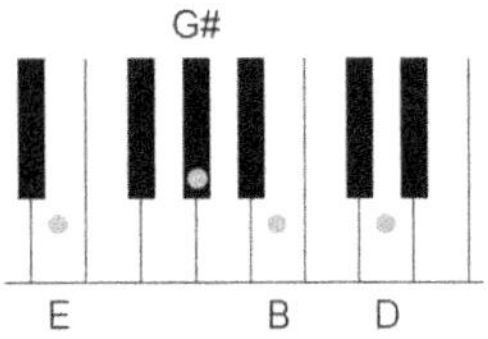

E7

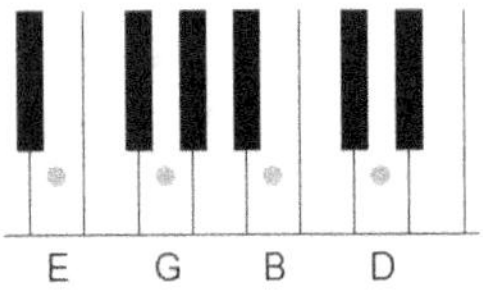

Em7

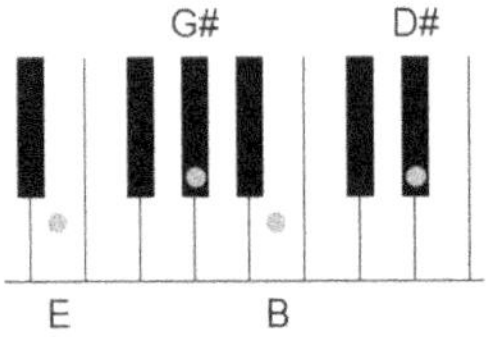

Emaj7

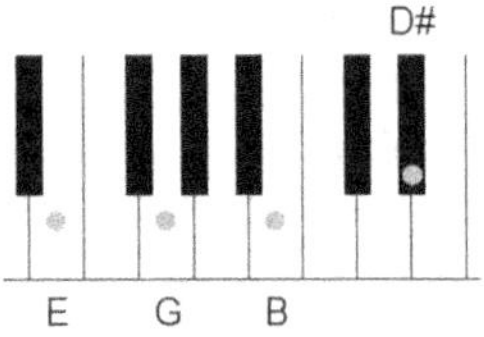

Emmaj7

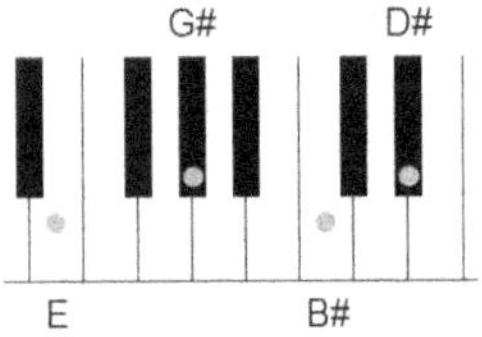

Emaj7+5

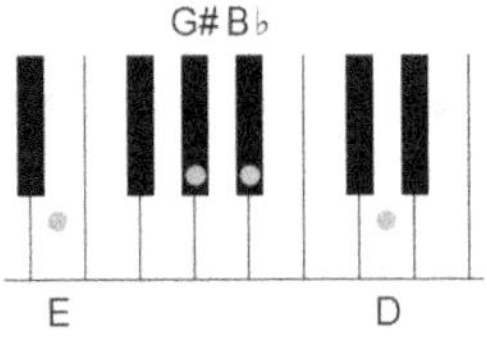

E7−5

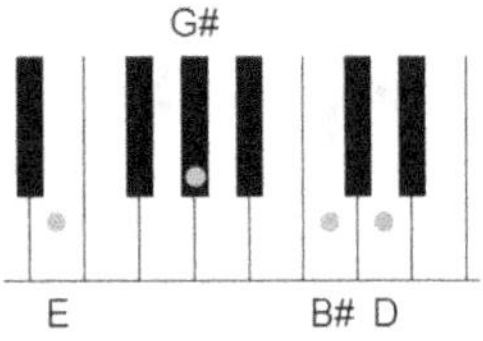

E7+5

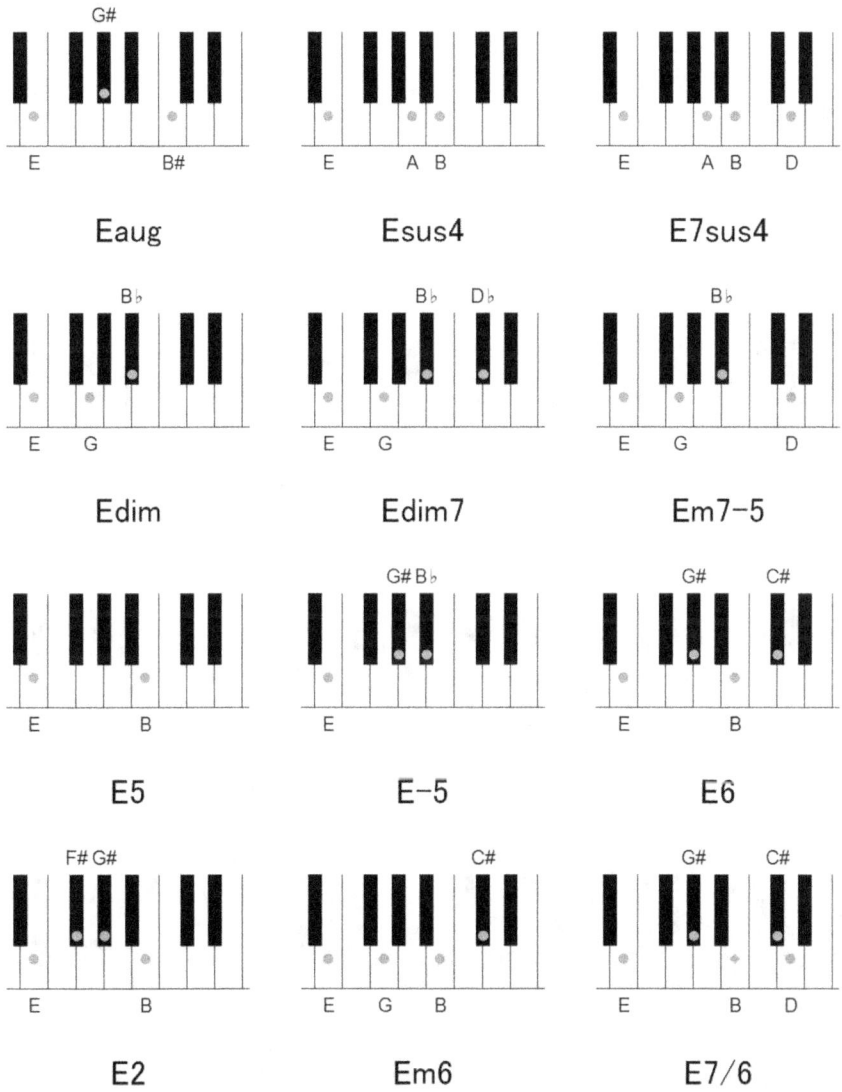

Eaug

Esus4

E7sus4

Edim

Edim7

Em7-5

E5

E-5

E6

E2

Em6

E7/6

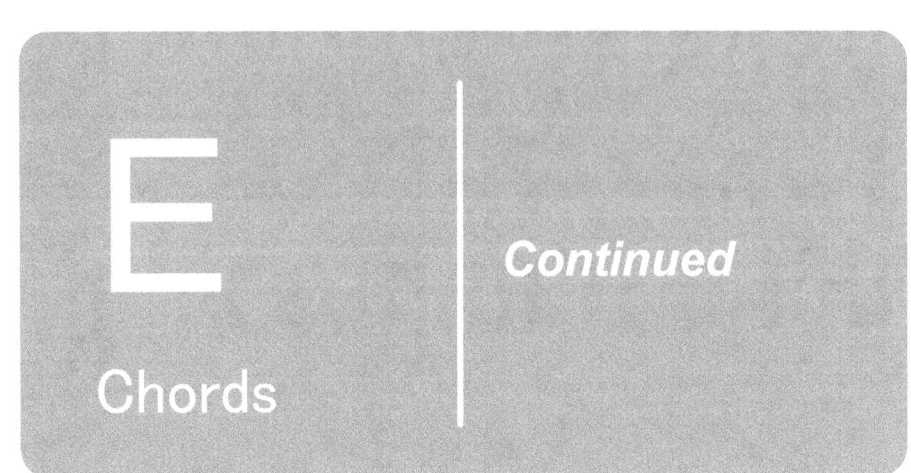

E

Continued

Chords

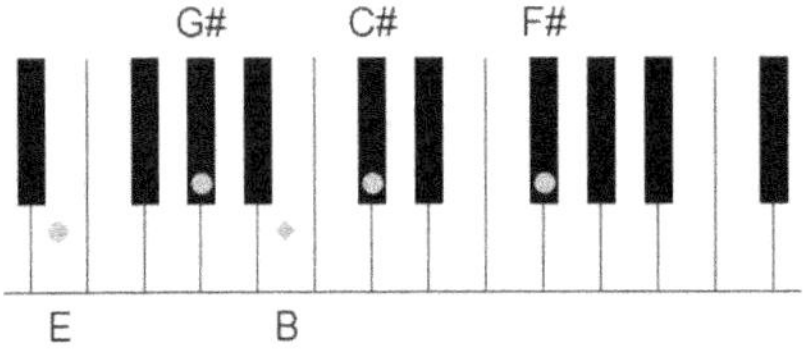

G# C# F#

E B

E6/9

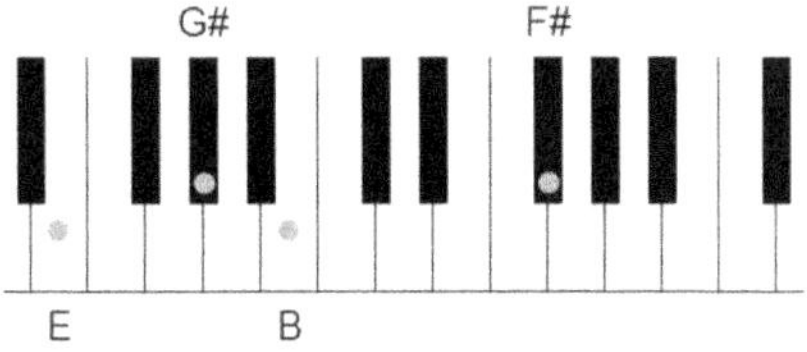

G# F#

E B

Eadd9

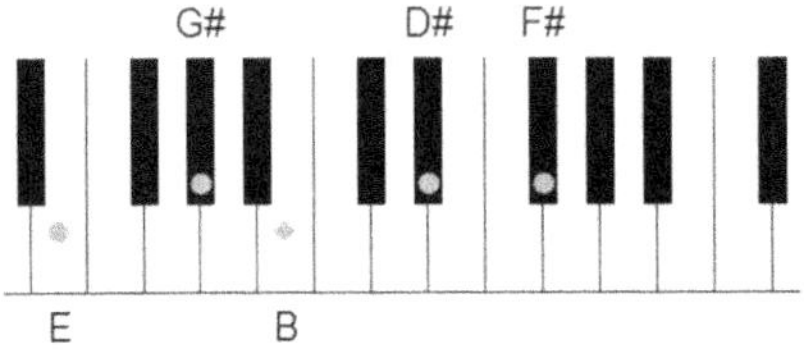

G# D# F#

E B

Emaj9

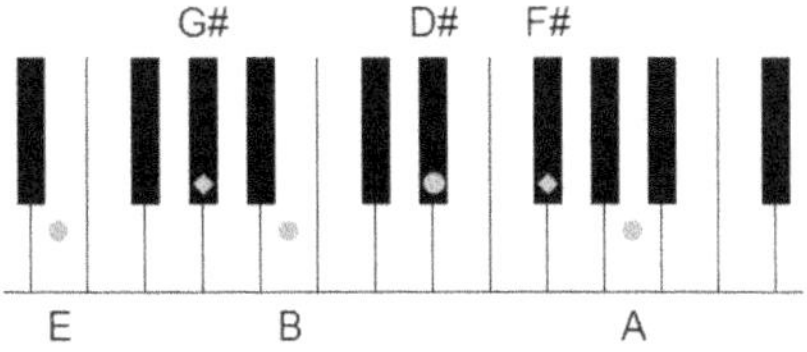

G# D# F#

E B A

Emaj11

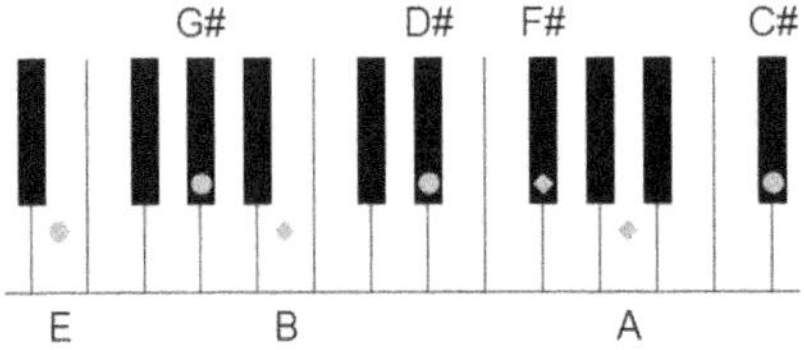

G# D# F# C#

E B A

Emaj13

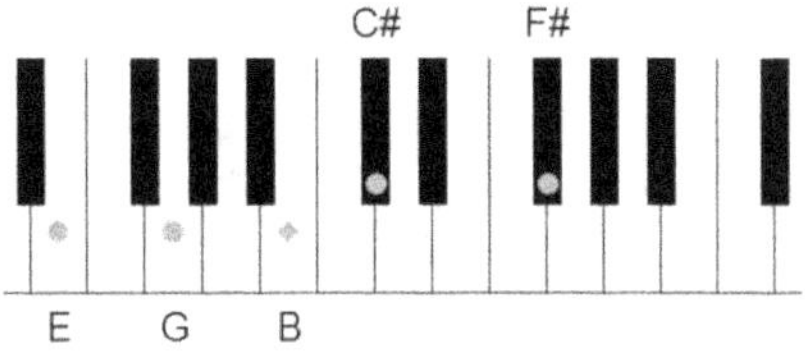

C# F#

E G B

Em6/9

Big Keyboard and Piano Chord Book
©2011 Moran Education http://www.MoranEducation.com/12Notes

E

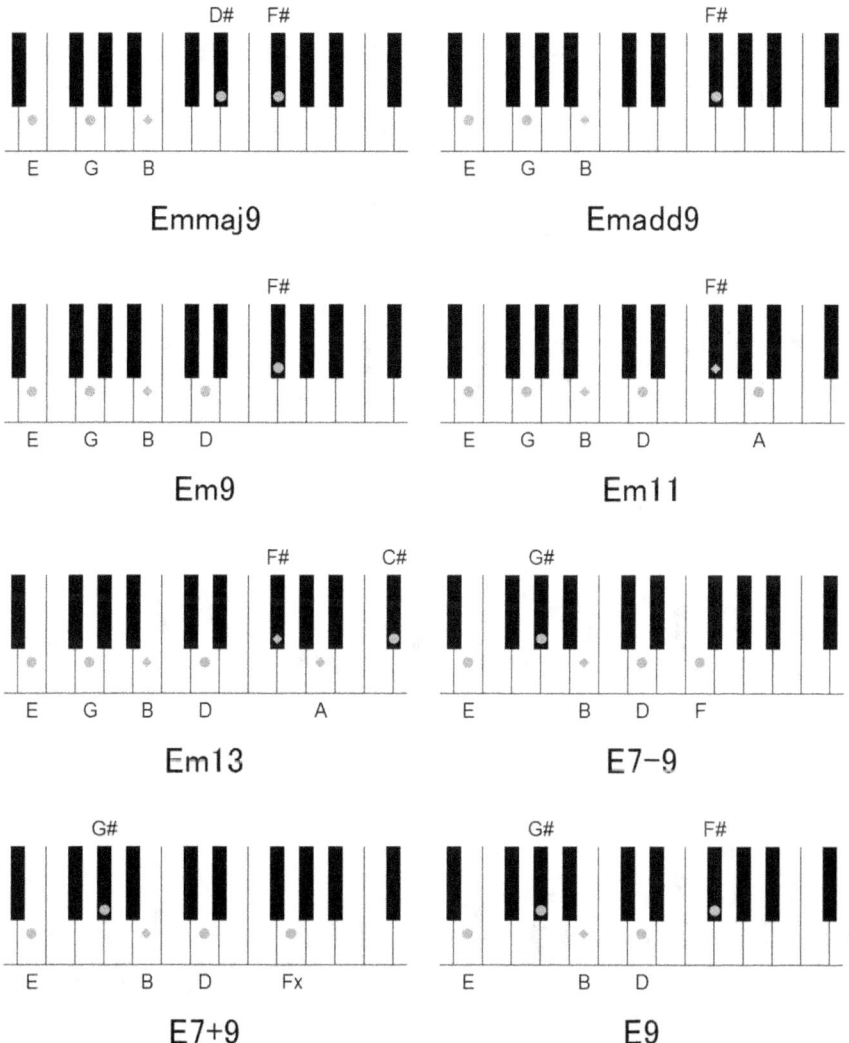

Emmaj9

Emadd9

Em9

Em11

Em13

E7−9

E7+9

E9

E
Chords

Continued

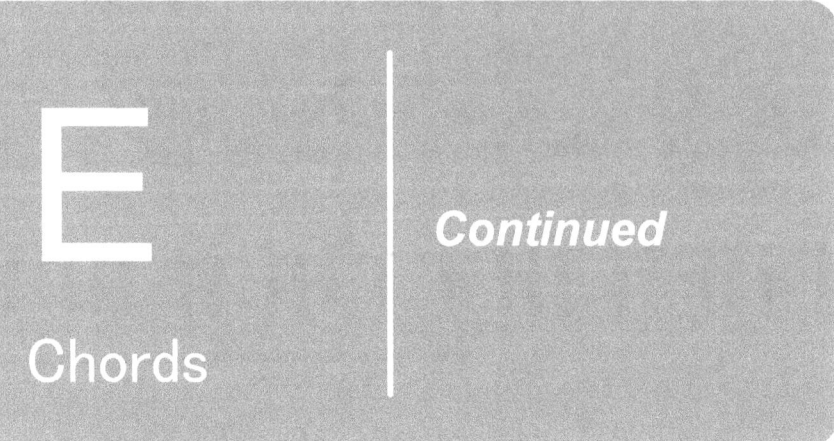

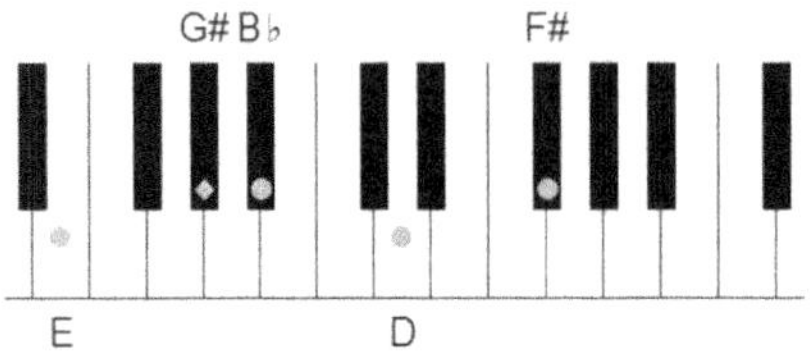

E9−5

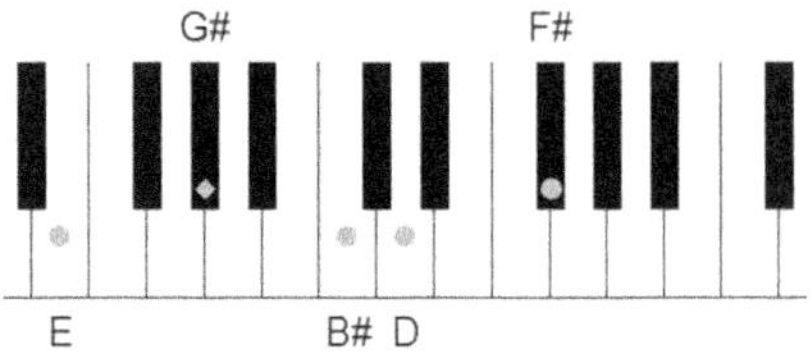

E9+5

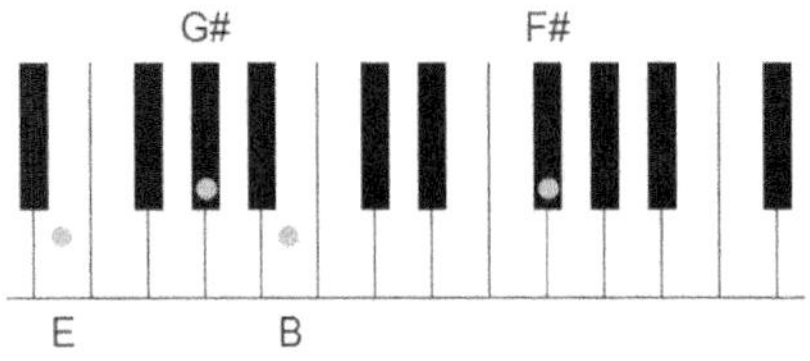

Eadd9

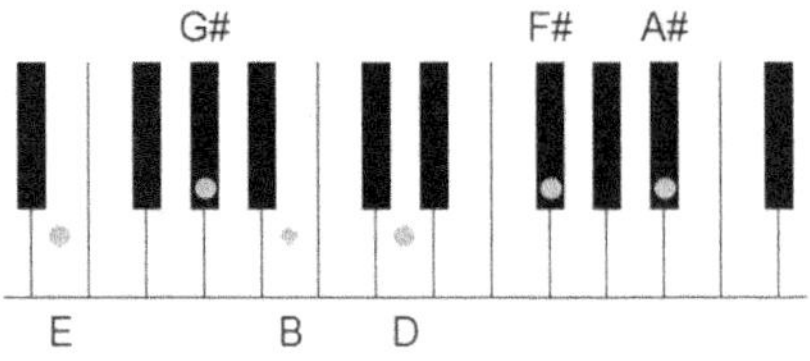

E9+11

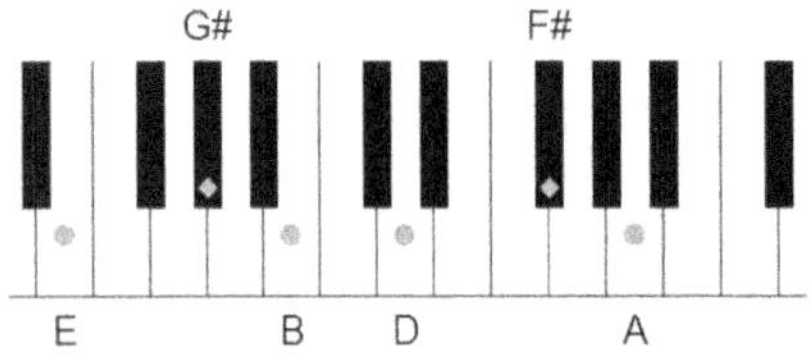

E11

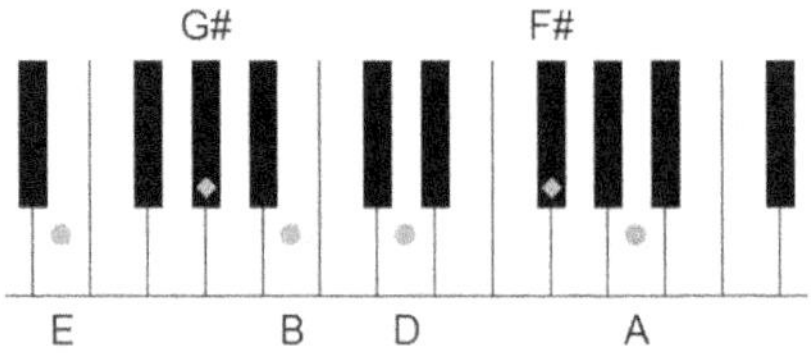

E11−9

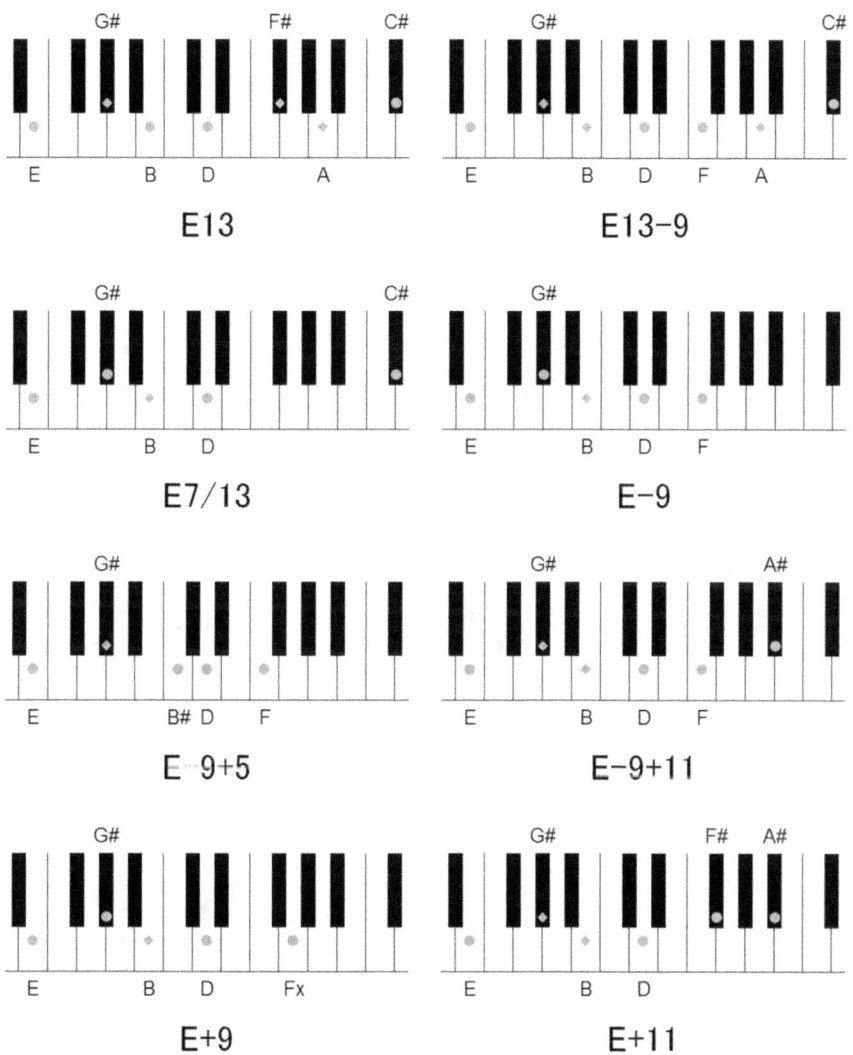

E13

E13-9

E7/13

E-9

E-9+5

E-9+11

E+9

E+11

F

Chords

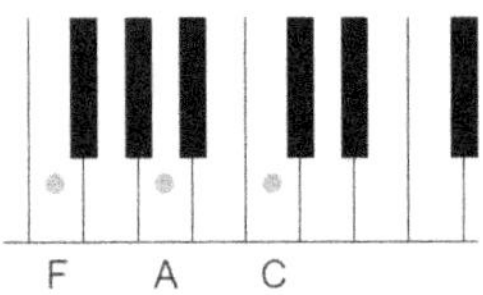

F Major

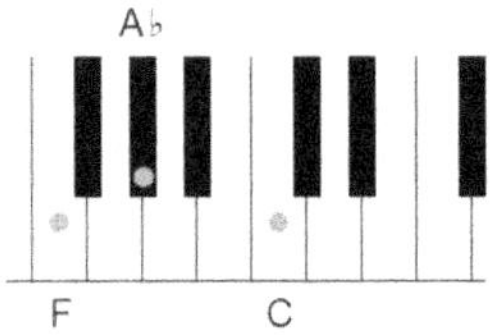

Fm

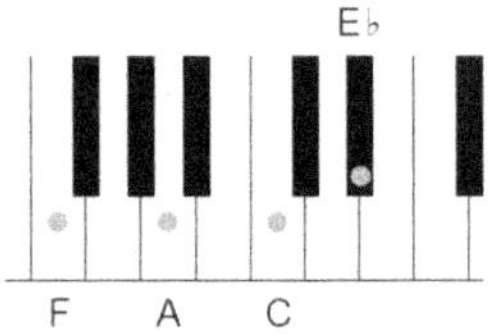

F7

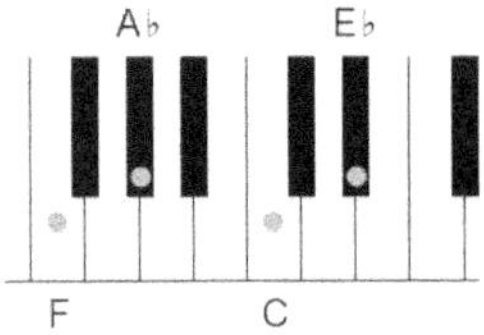

Fm7

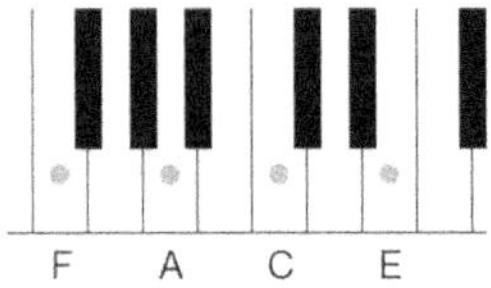

Fmaj7

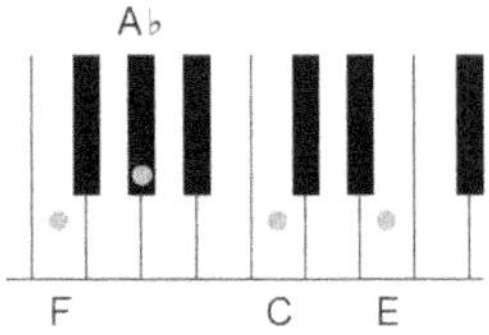

Fmmaj7

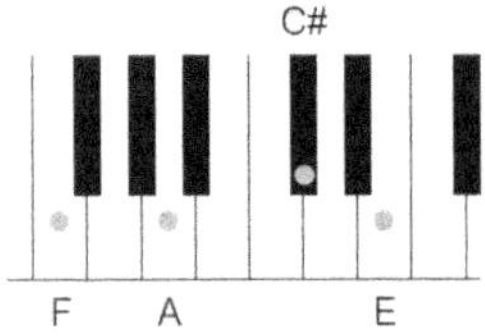

Fmaj7+5

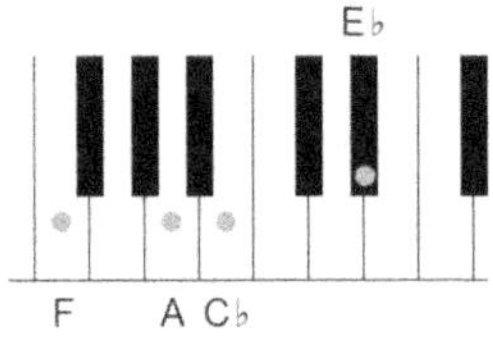

F7-5

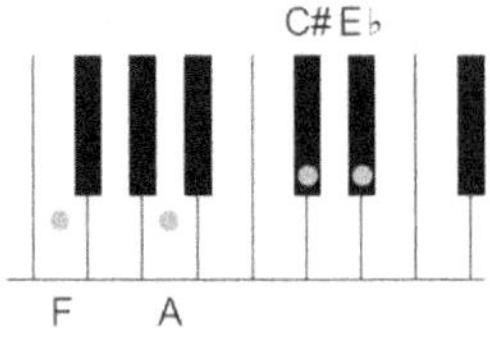

F7+5

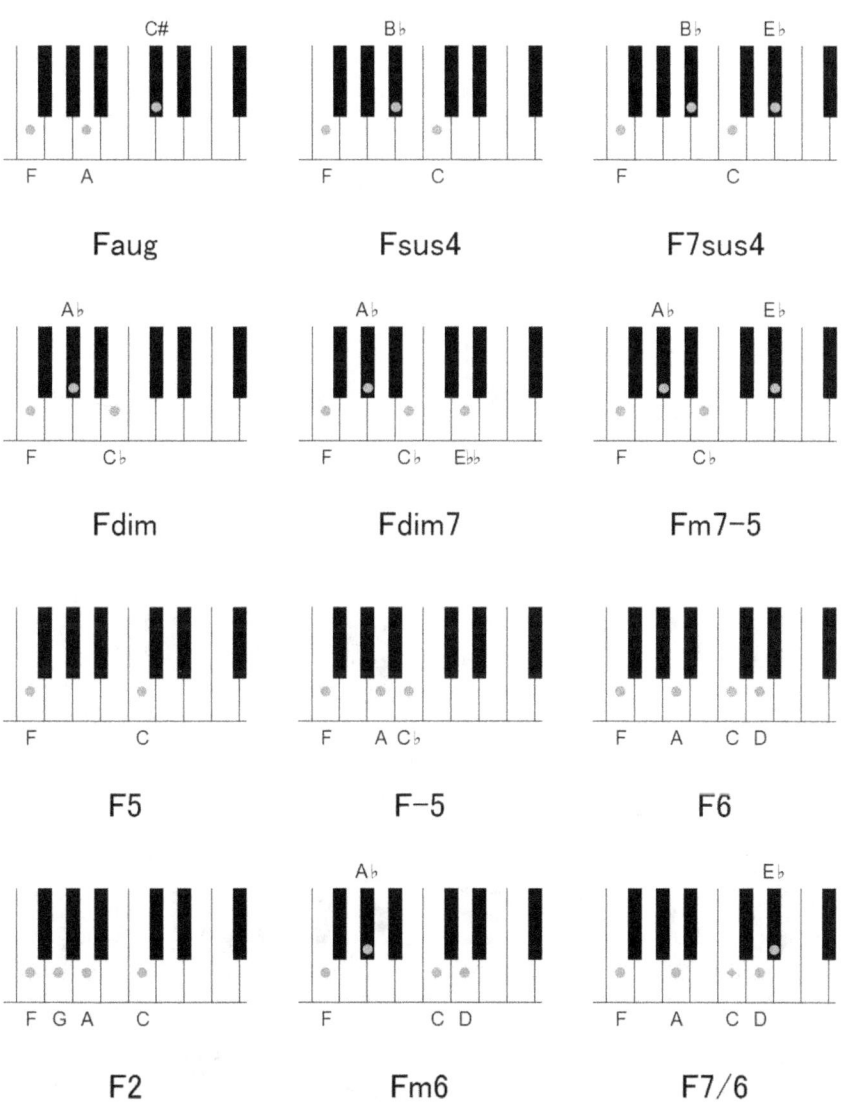

Faug   Fsus4   F7sus4

Fdim   Fdim7   Fm7−5

F5   F−5   F6

F2   Fm6   F7/6

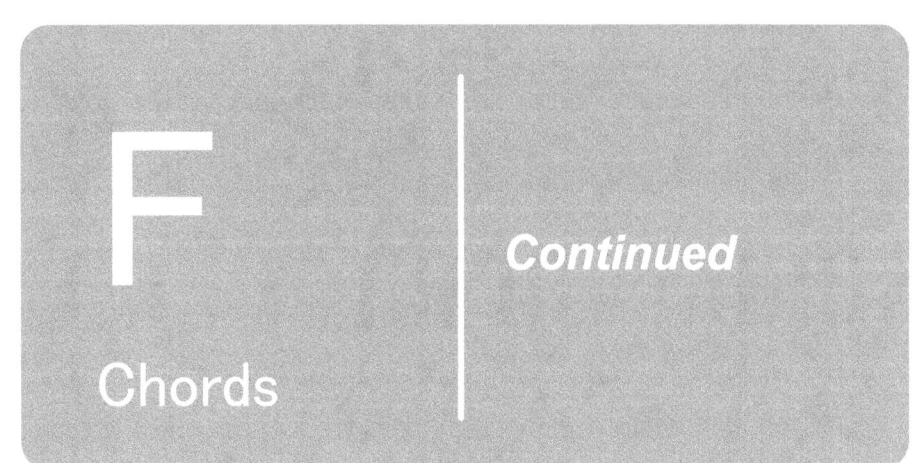

F

Chords

Continued

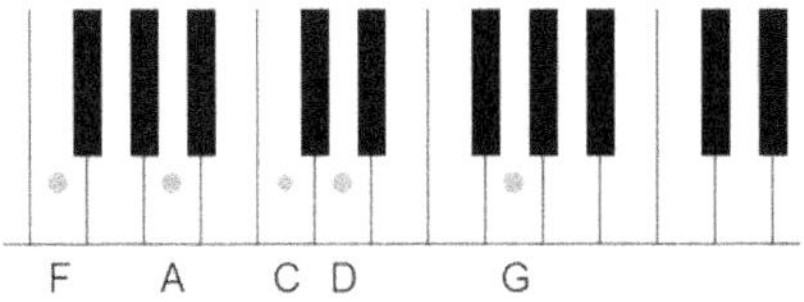

F6/9

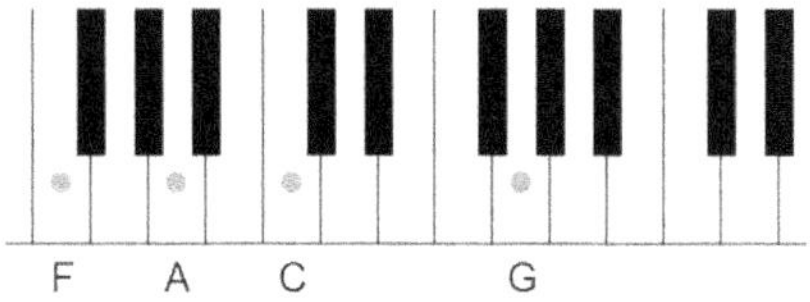

Fadd9

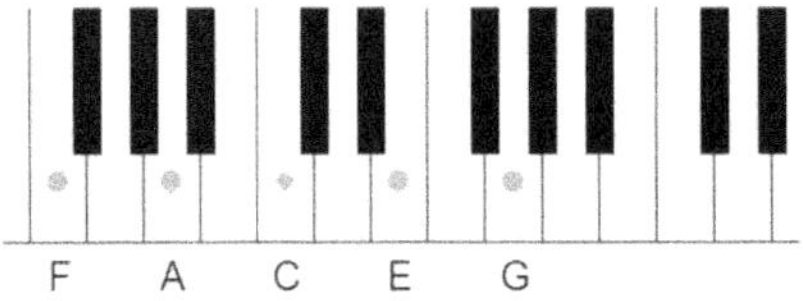

Fmaj9

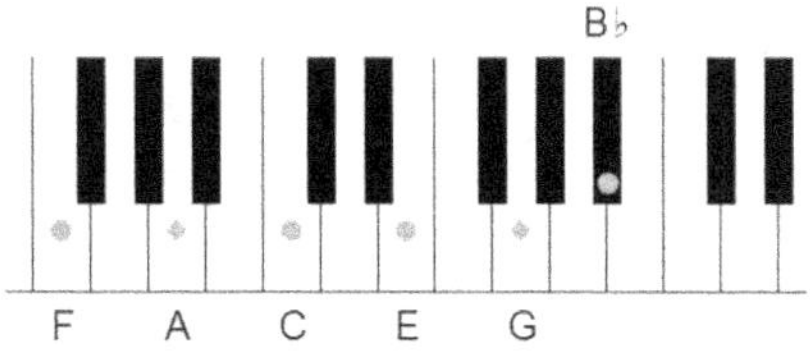

Fmaj11

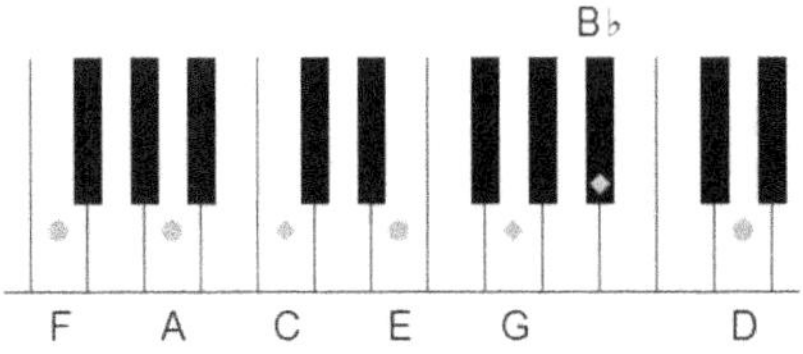

Fmaj13

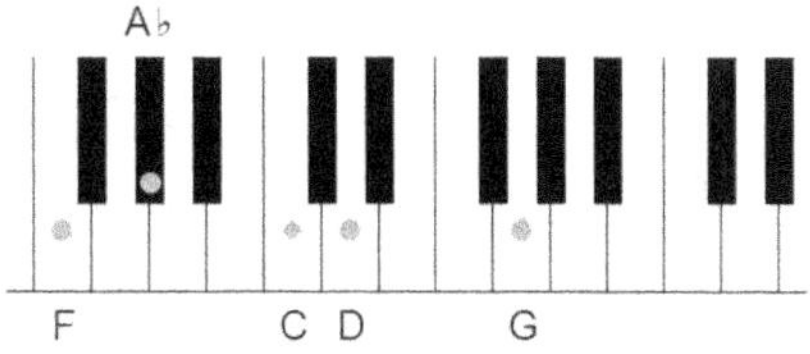

Fm6/9

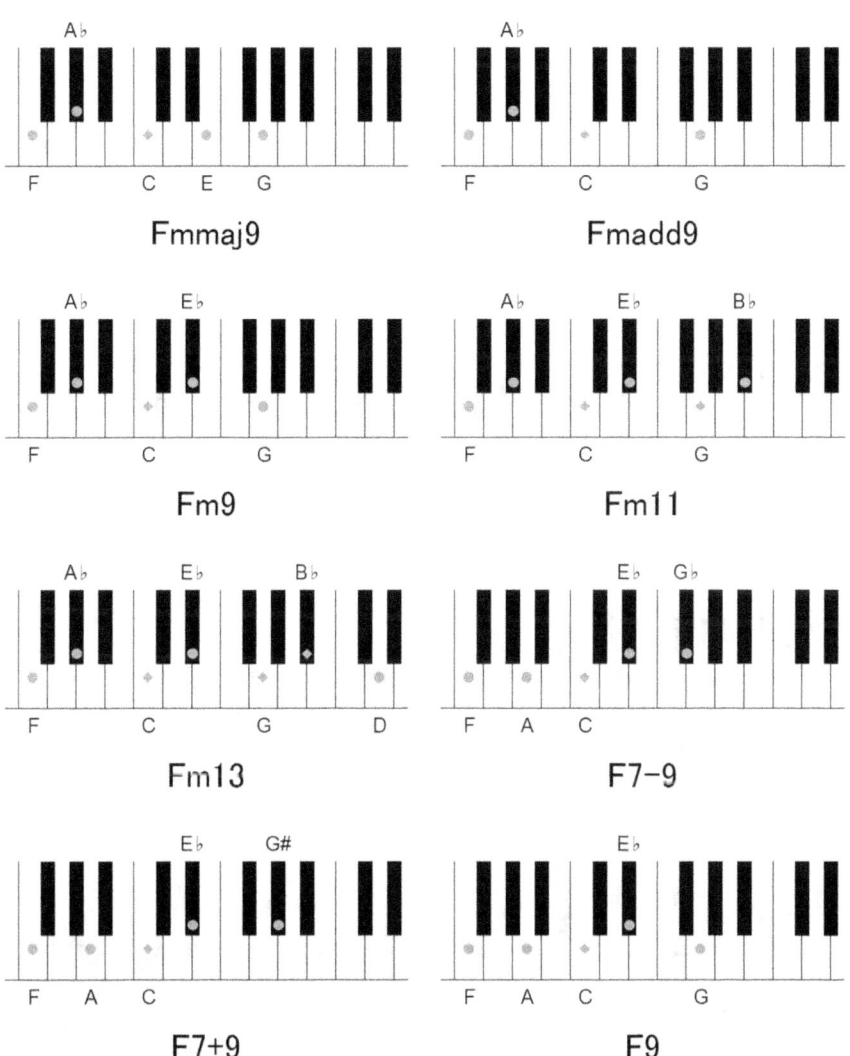

Fmmaj9

Fmadd9

Fm9

Fm11

Fm13

F7−9

F7+9

F9

Big Keyboard and Piano Chord Book

©2011 Moran Education http://www.MoranEducation.com/12Notes

F Chords

Continued

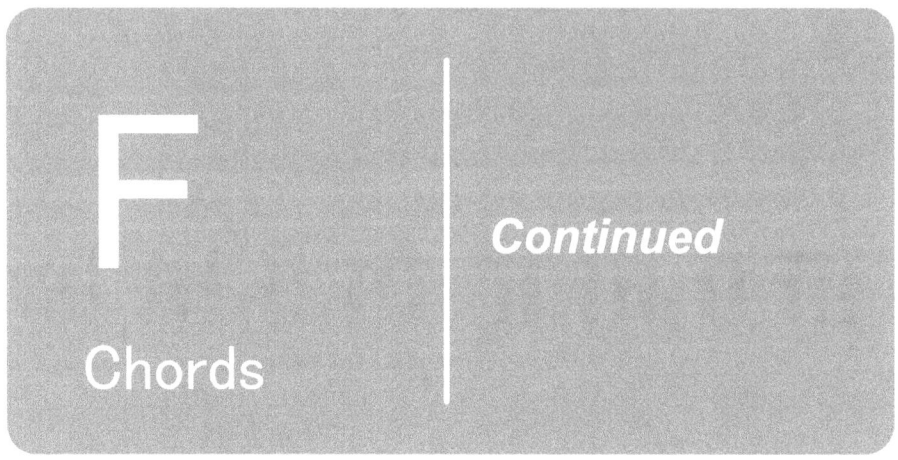

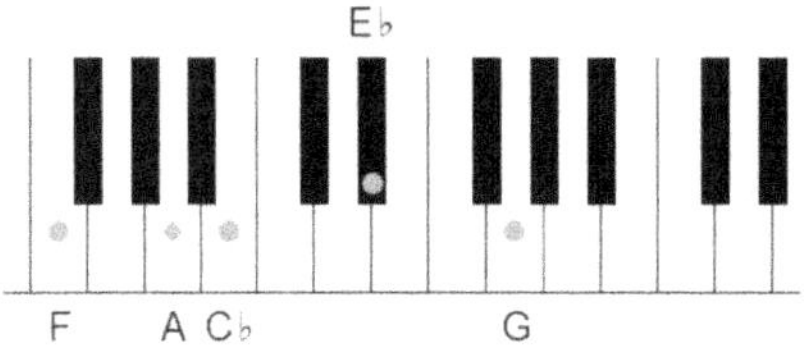

F9-5

F9+5

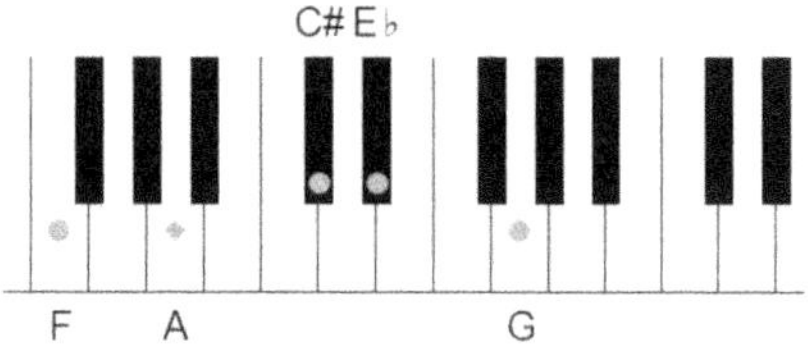

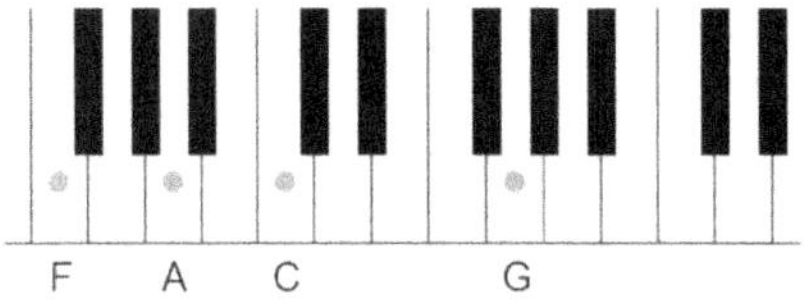

Fadd9

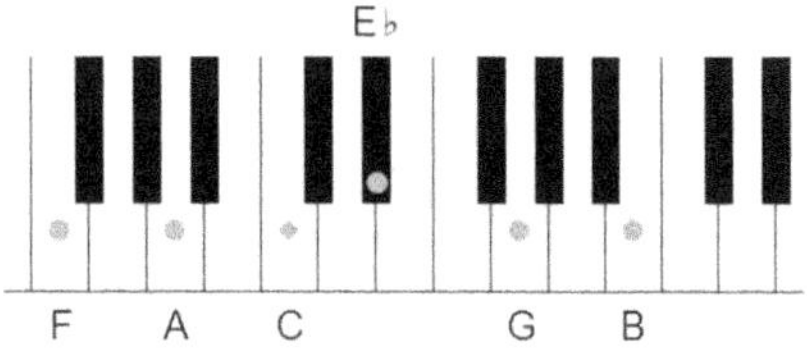

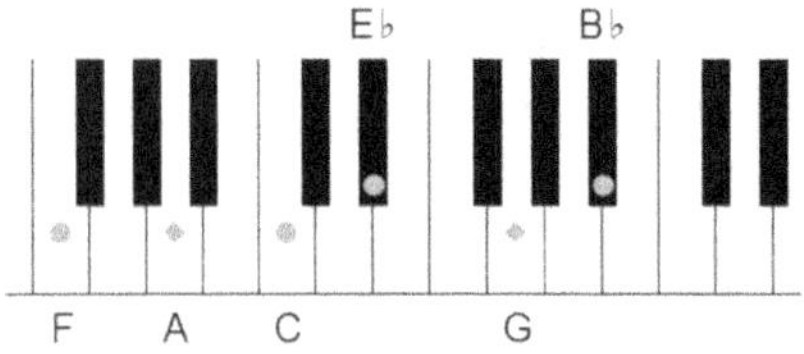

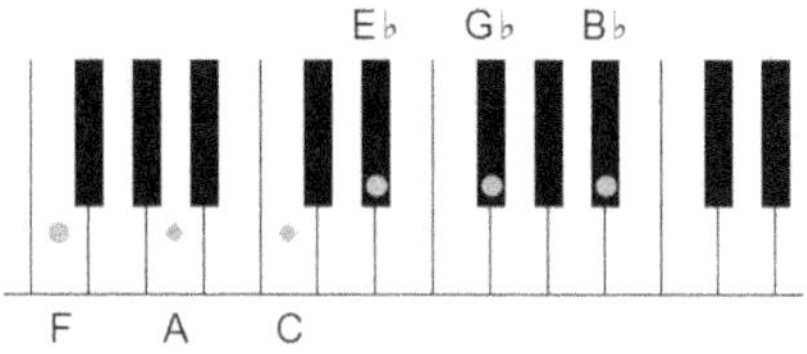

F9+11

F11

F11-9

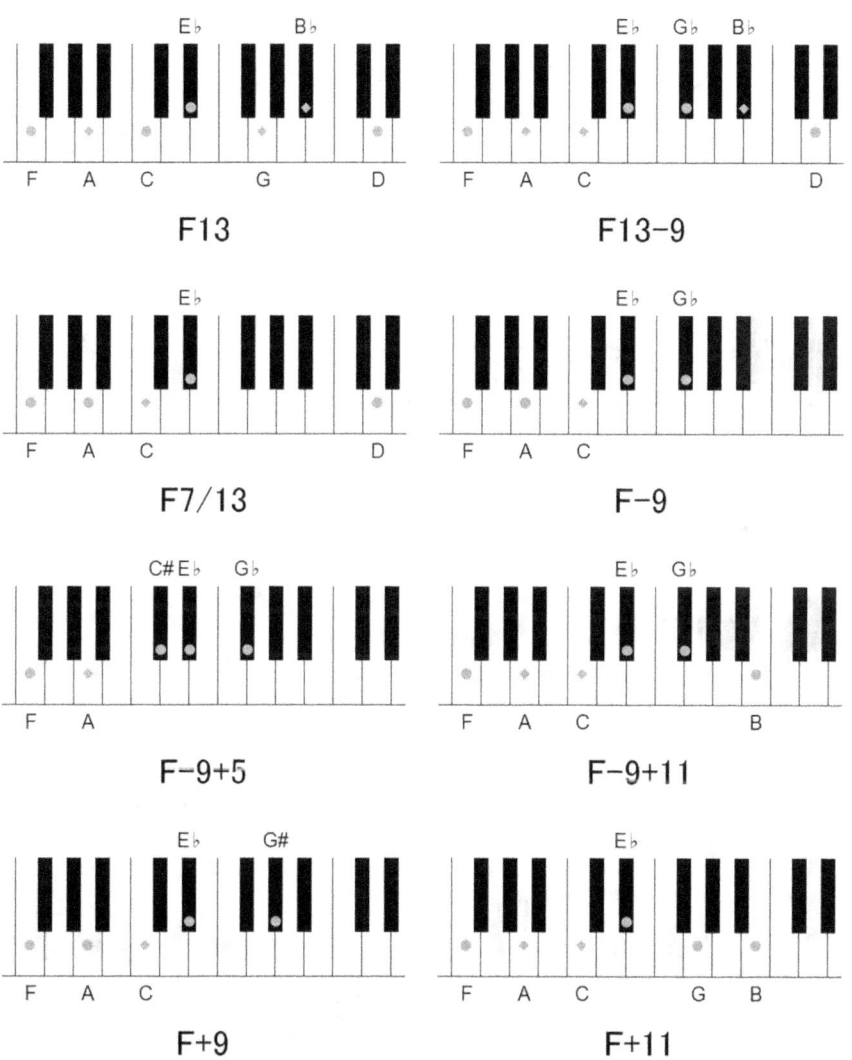

F13

F13-9

F7/13

F-9

F-9+5

F-9+11

F+9

F+11

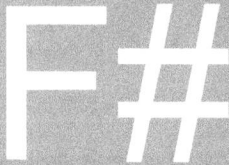

F#

F# is also known as G♭

Chords

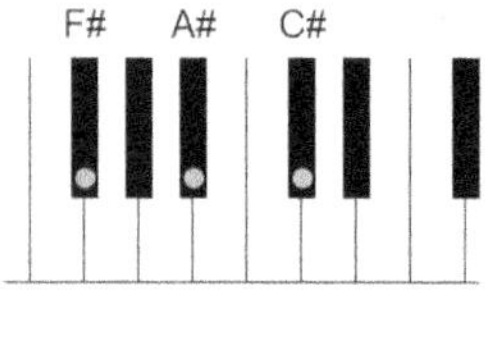

F# A# C#	F# C#	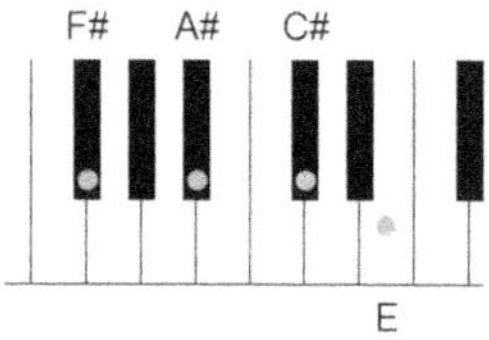 F# A# C#
	A	E
F# Major	**F#m**	**F#7**

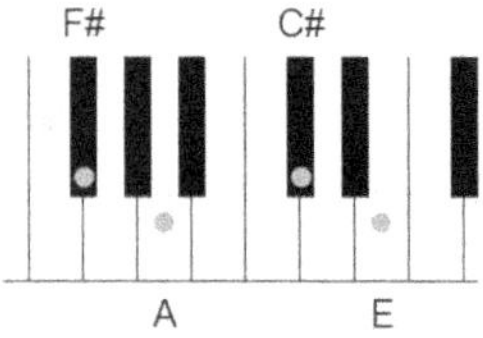 F# C#	F# A# C#	F# C#
A E	E#	A E#
F#m7	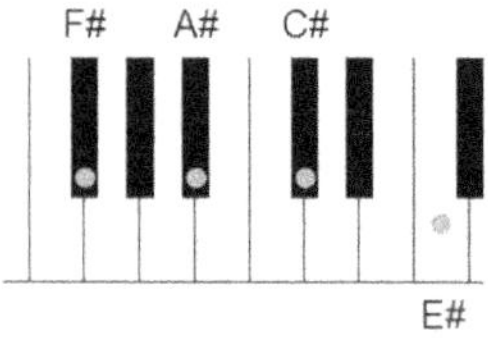 **F#maj7**	**F#mmaj7**

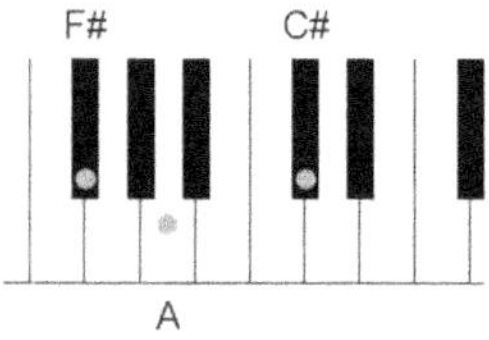

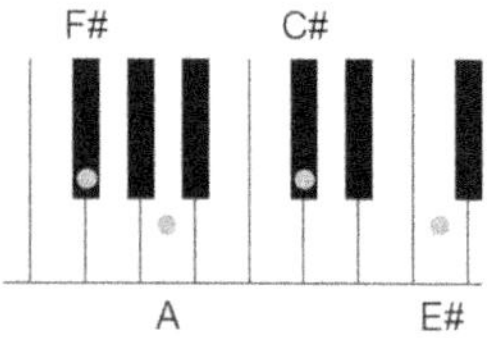

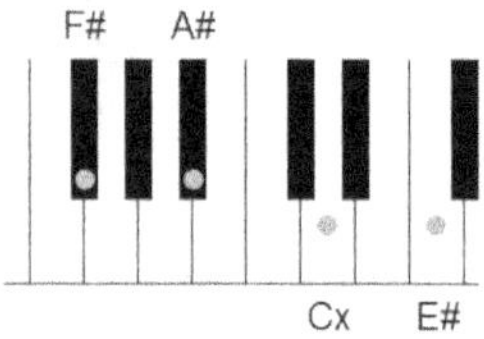 F# A#	F# A#	F# A#
Cx E#	C E	Cx E
F#maj7+5	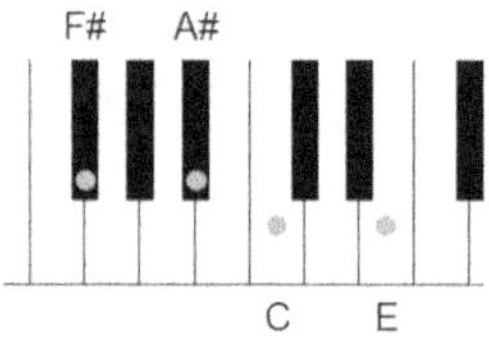 **F#7-5**	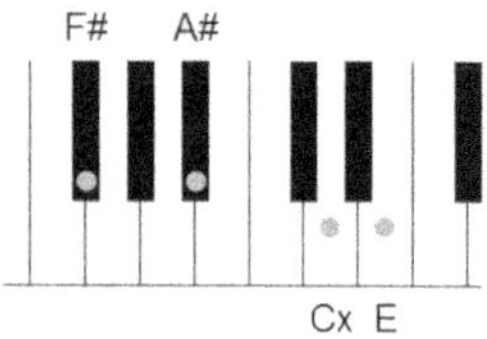 **F#7+5**

Big Keyboard and Piano Chord Book
©2011 Moran Education http://www.MoranEducation.com/12Notes

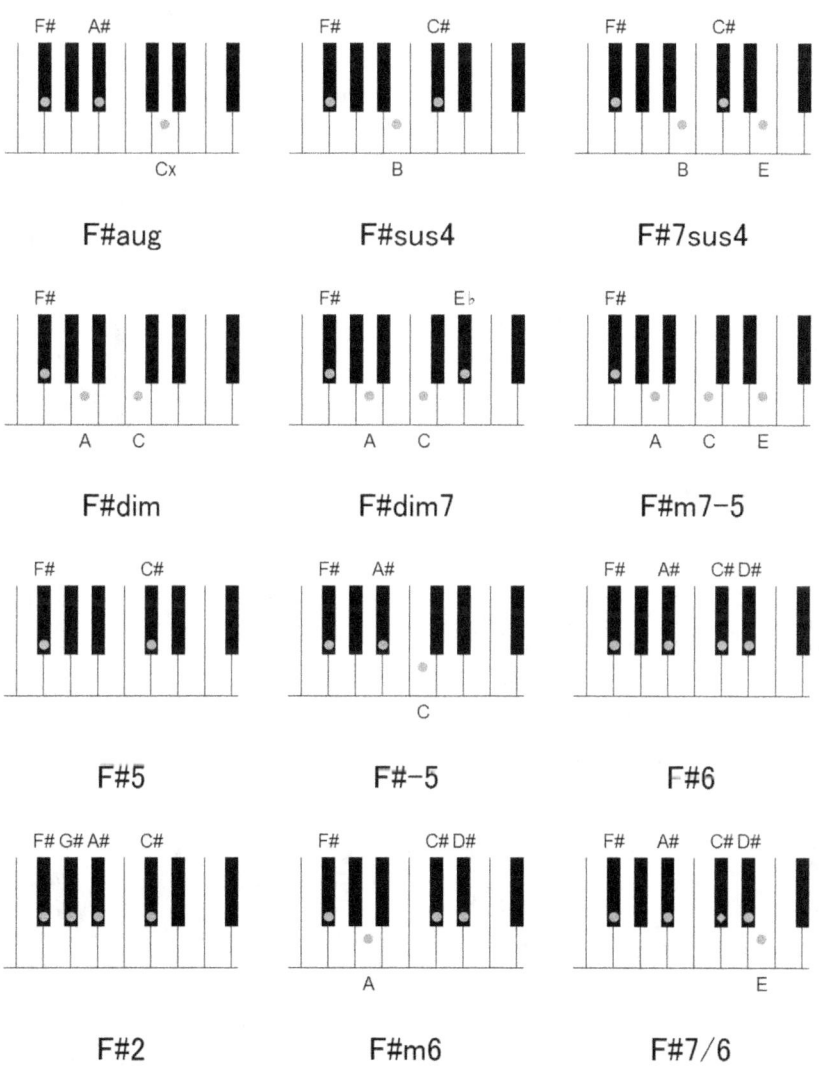

F#aug

F#sus4

F#7sus4

F#dim

F#dim7

F#m7-5

F#5

F#-5

F#6

F#2

F#m6

F#7/6

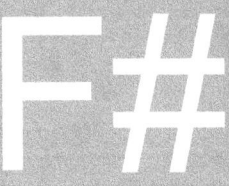

F# Chords | *Continued*

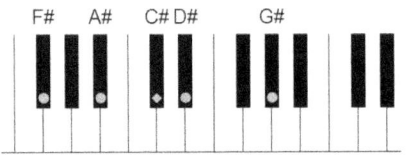

F#6/9

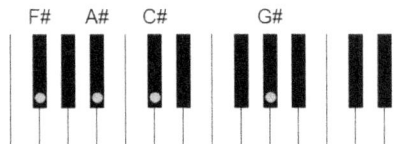

F#add9

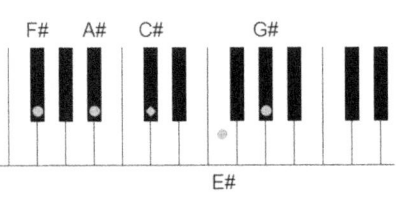

F#maj9

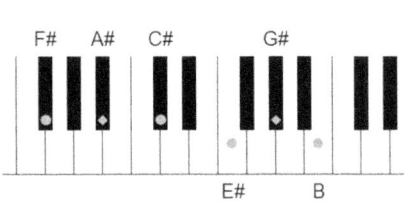

F#maj11

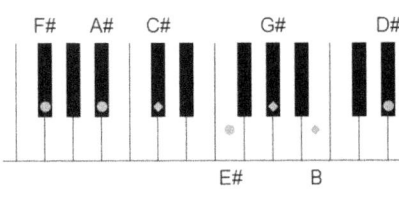

F#maj13

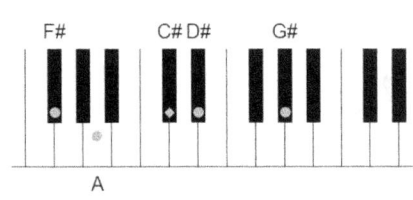

F#m6/9

Big Keyboard and Piano Chord Book

©2011 Moran Education http://www.MoranEducation.com/12Notes

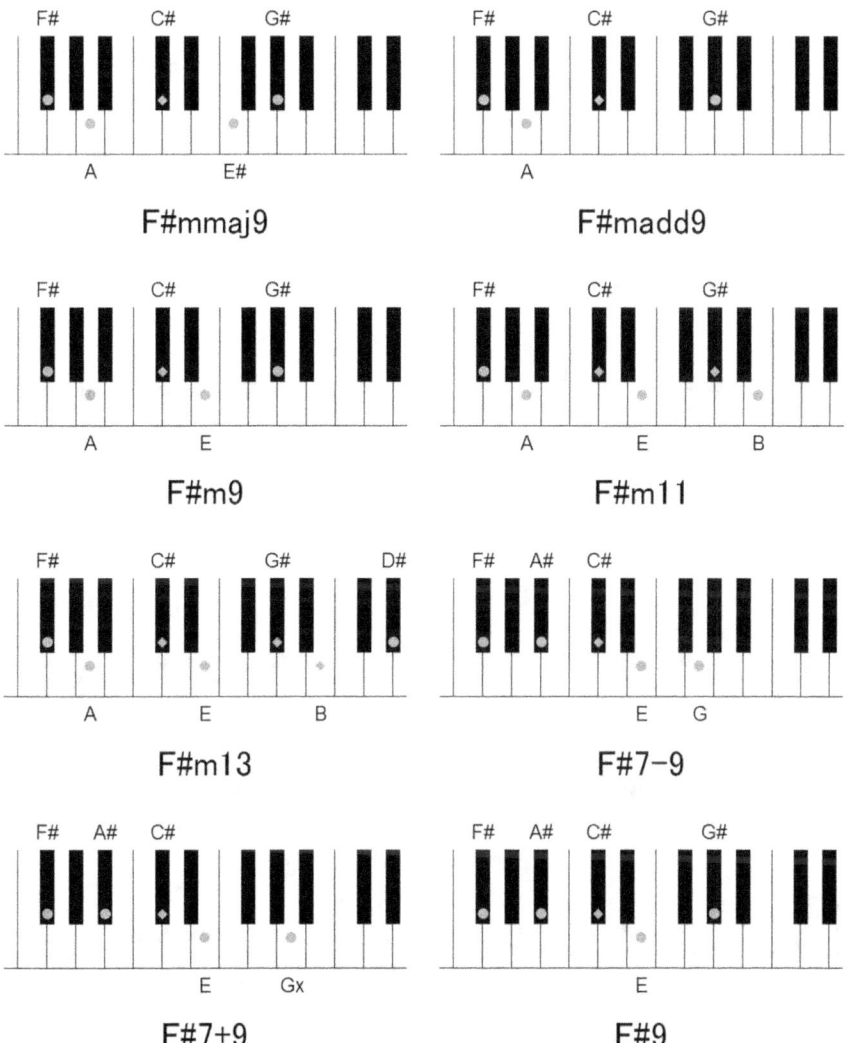

F#mmaj9

F#madd9

F#m9

F#m11

F#m13

F#7-9

F#7+9

F#9

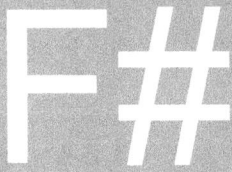

F# Continued

Chords

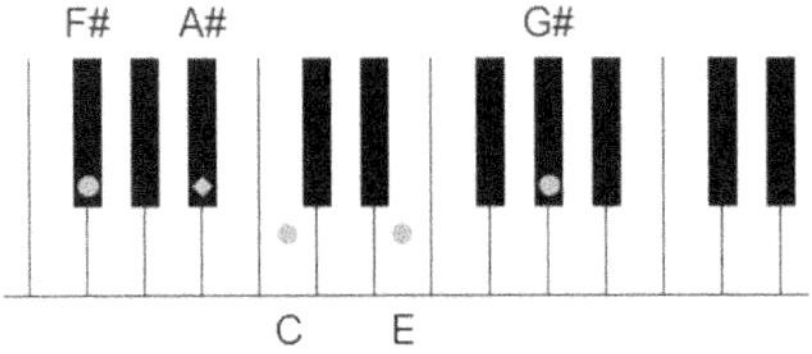

F#9-5

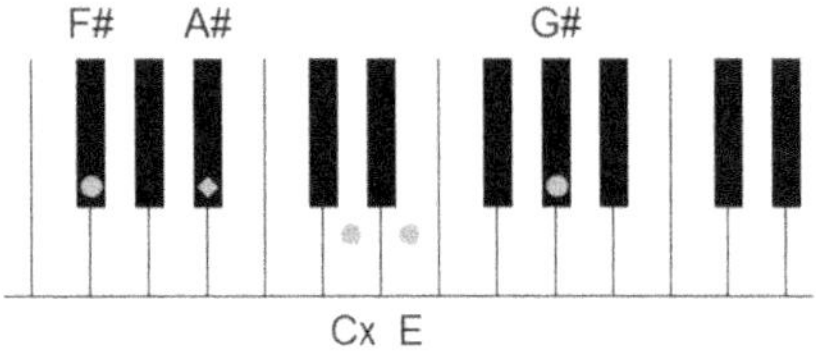

F# A# C E G#

F#9+5

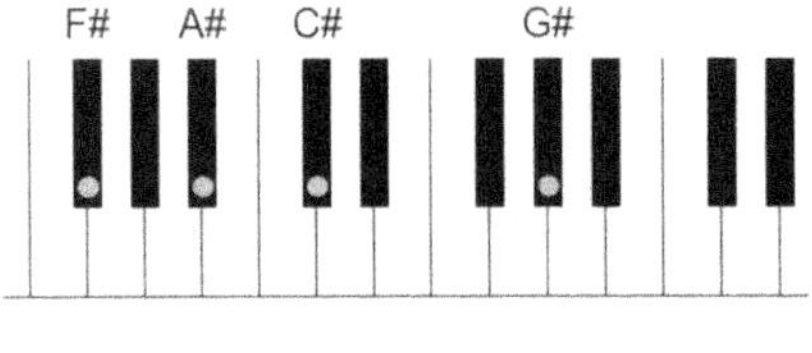

F# A# Cx E G#

F#add9

F# A# C# G#

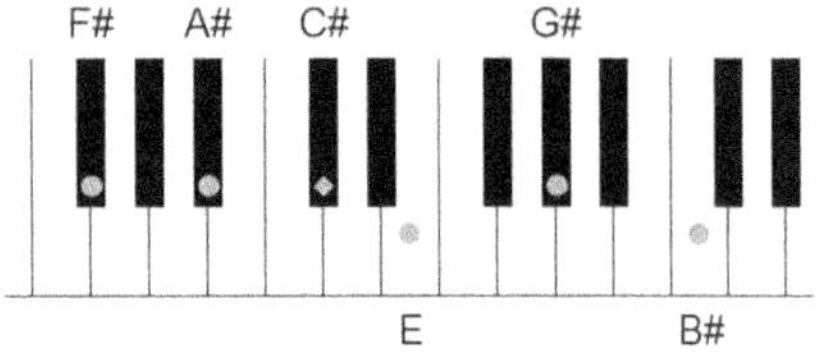

F#9+11

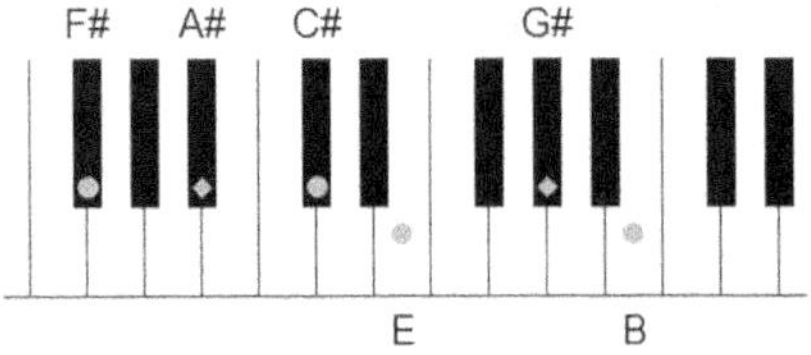

F# A# C# E G# B#

F#11

F# A# C# E G# B

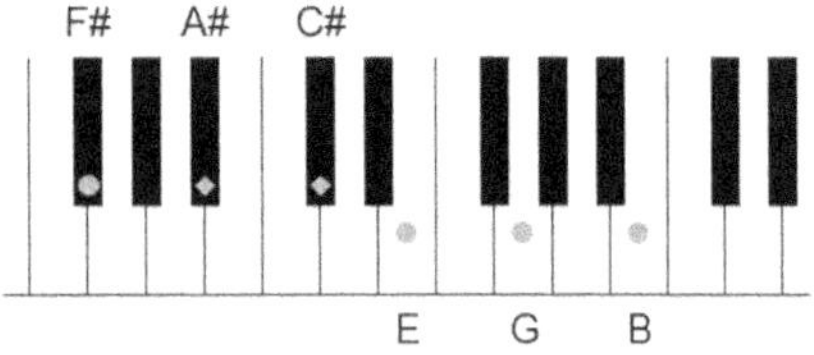

F#11-9

F# A# C# E G B

F#

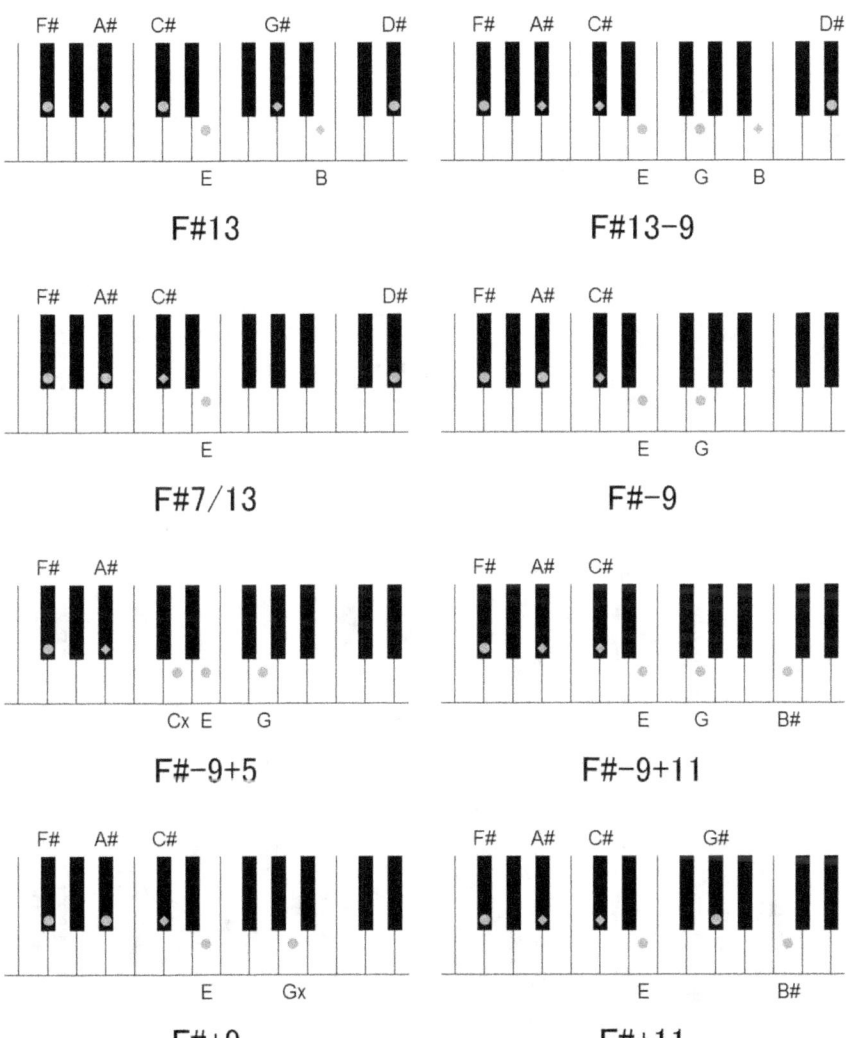

F#13

F#13-9

F#7/13

F#-9

F#-9+5

F#-9+11

F#+9

F#+11

G

Chords

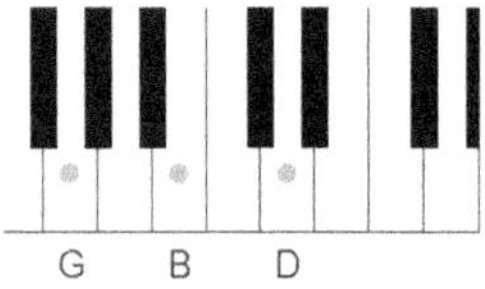

G Major	Gm	G7
Gm7	Gmaj7	Gmmaj7
Gmaj7+5	G7-5	G7+5

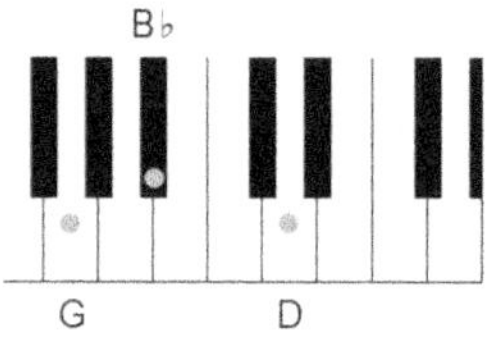

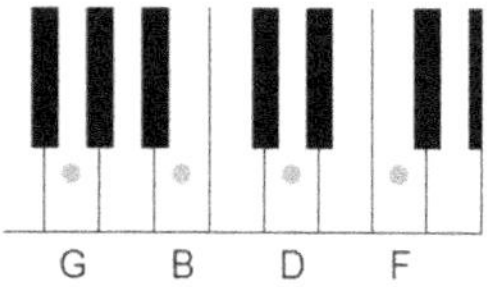

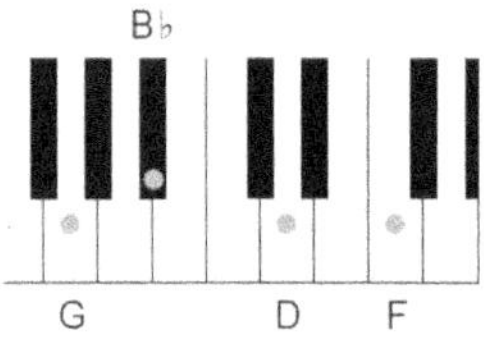

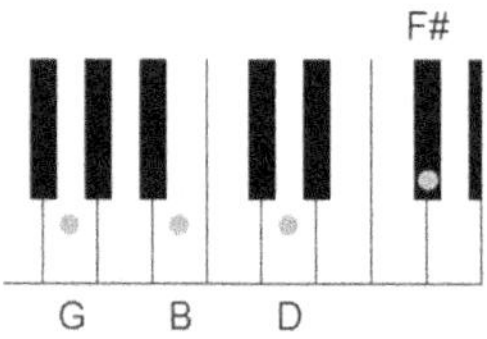

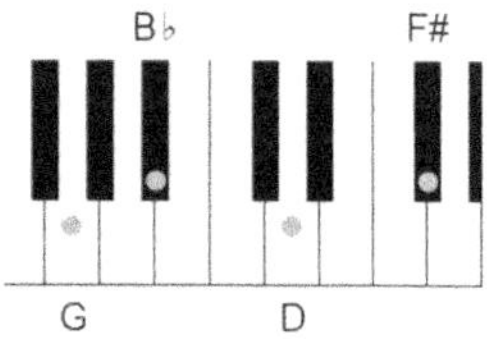

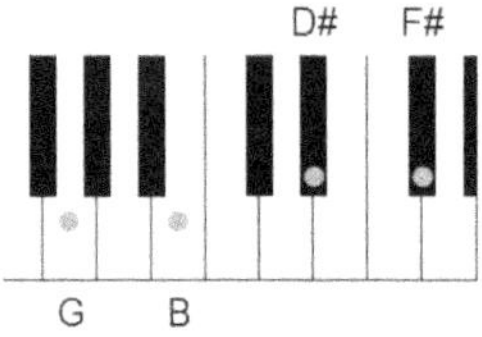

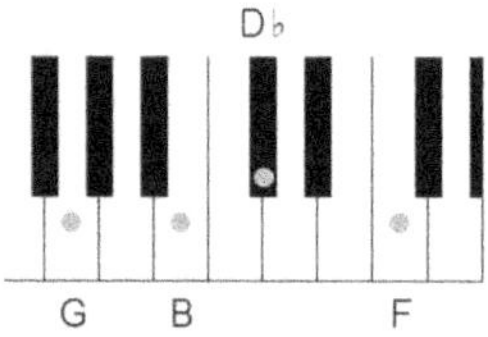

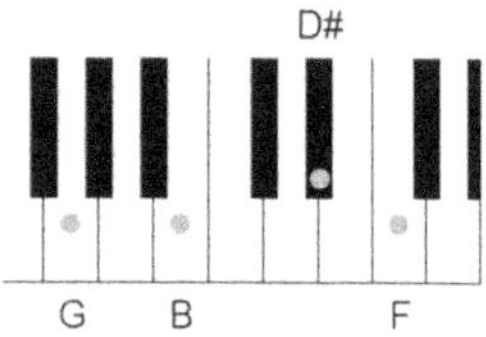

Big Keyboard and Piano Chord Book
©2011 Moran Education http://www.MoranEducation.com/12Notes

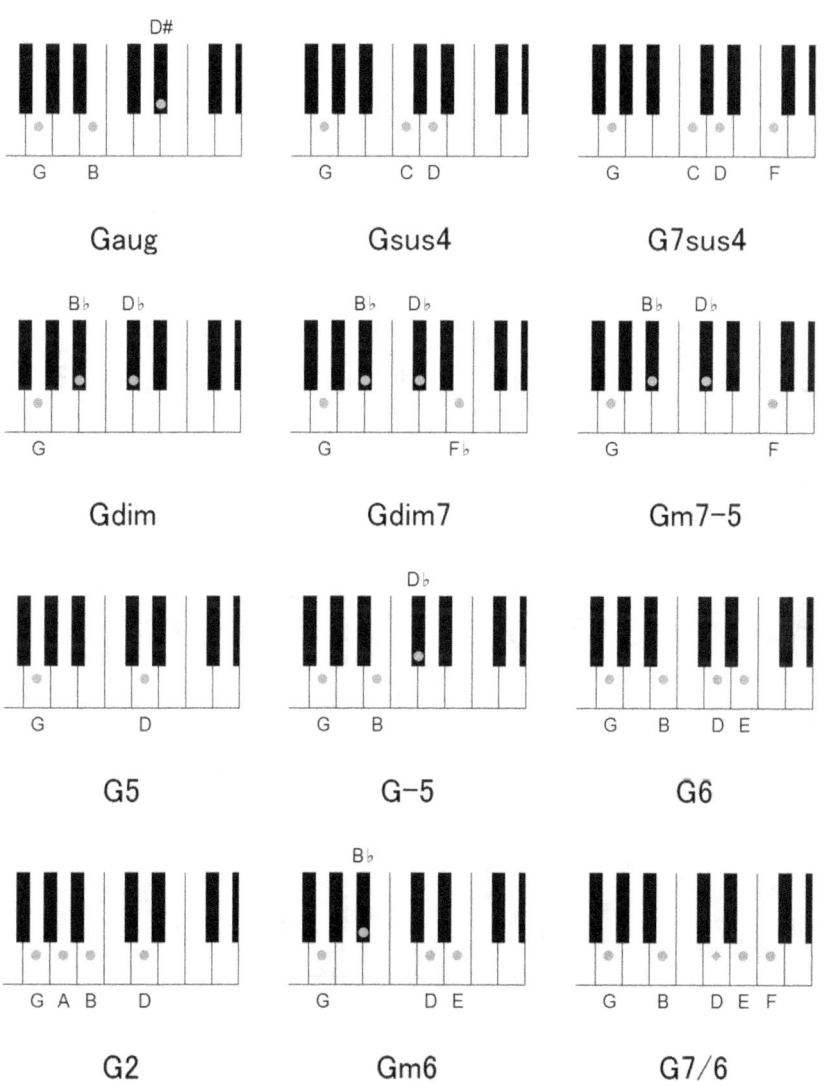

Gaug

Gsus4

G7sus4

Gdim

Gdim7

Gm7−5

G5

G−5

G6

G2

Gm6

G7/6

G

Continued

Chords

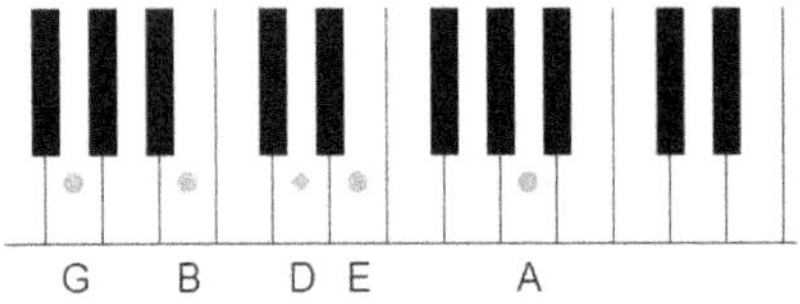

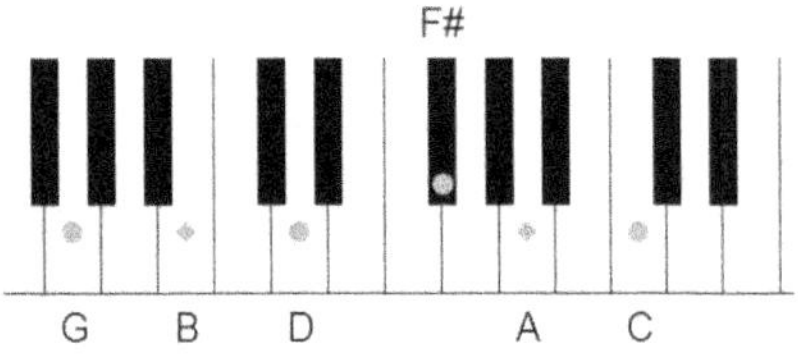

G6/9

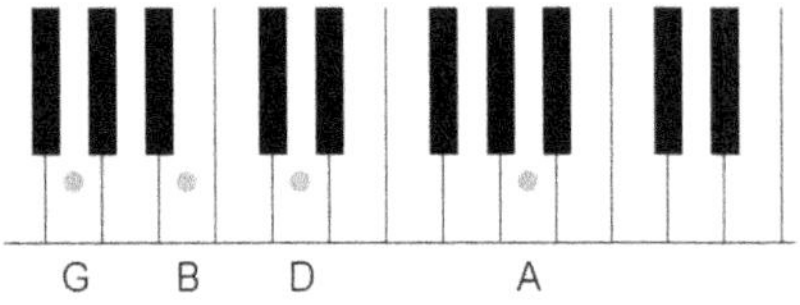

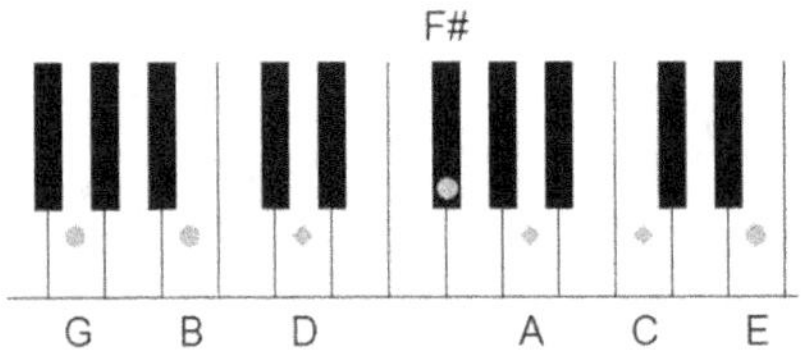

Gadd9

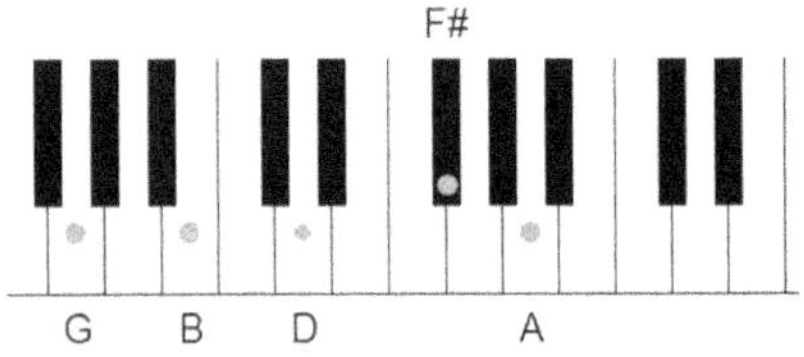

Gmaj9

Gmaj11

Gmaj13

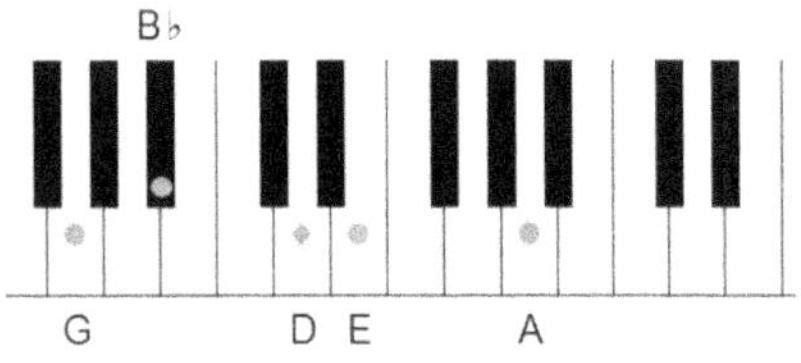

Gm6/9

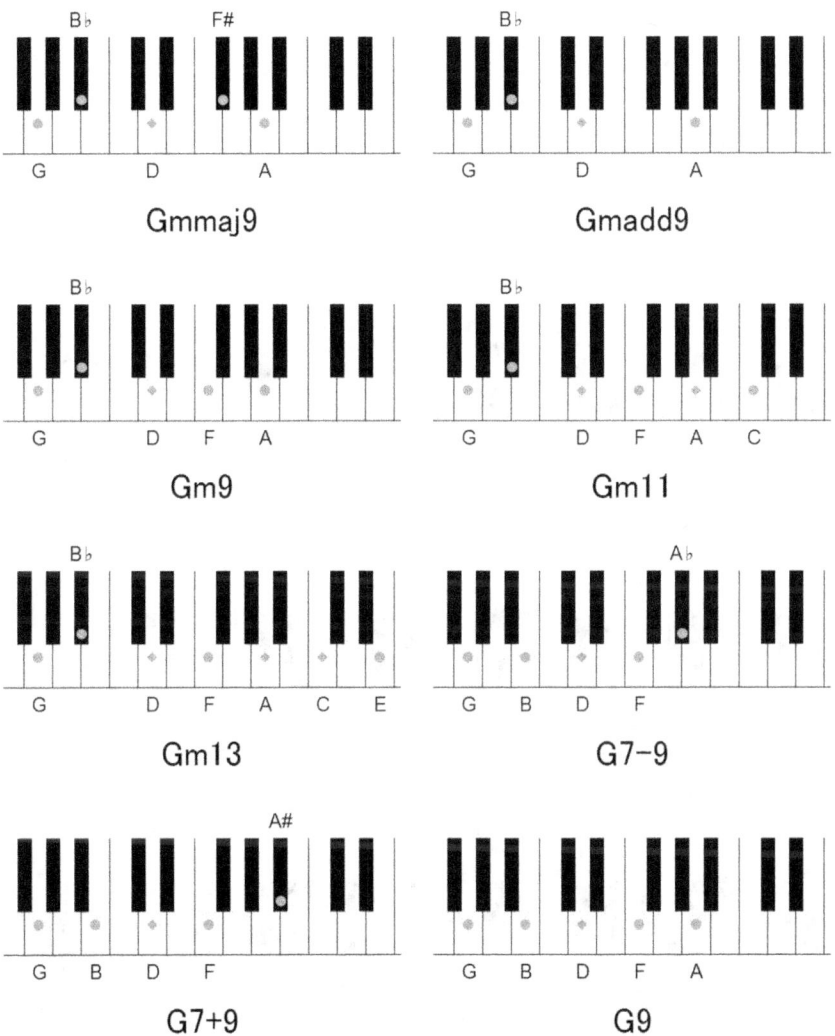

Gmmaj9

Gmadd9

Gm9

Gm11

Gm13

G7−9

G7+9

G9

G

Continued

Chords

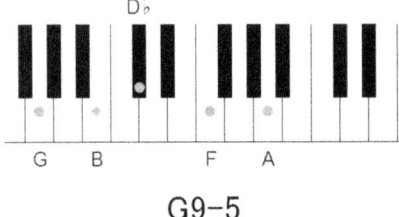

G9-5

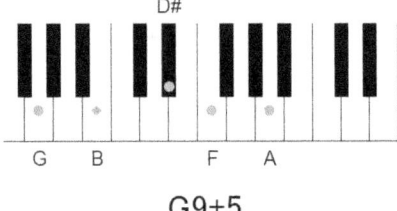

G9+5

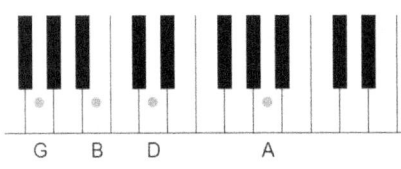

Gadd9

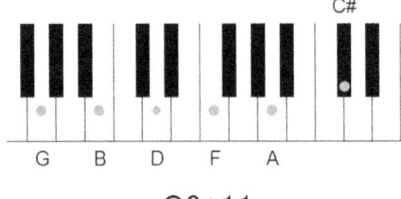

G9+11

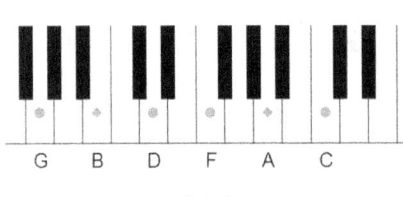

G11

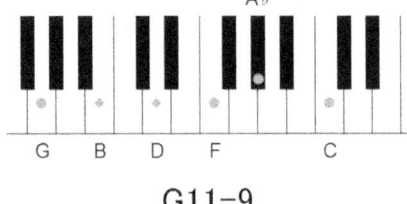

G11-9

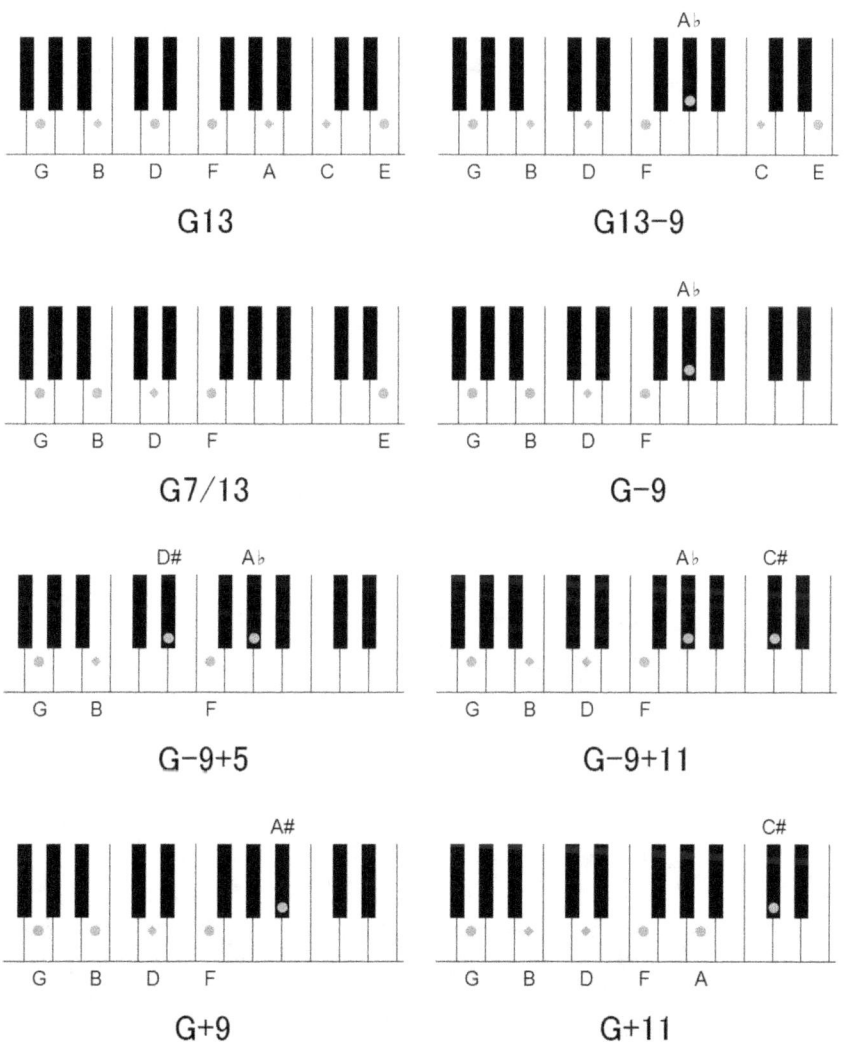

G13

G13-9

G7/13

G-9

G-9+5

G-9+11

G+9

G+11

Index

Find Stuff

12 Notes

View more products in our range, and download free resources for keyboard and piano at our website.

www.MoranEducation.com/12Notes

12 Notes - Big Keyboard and Piano Chord Book
Edition I

www.MoranEducation.com/12Notes

ISBN 978-1-4710-1495-6

www.ingramcontent.com/pod-product-compliance
Lightning Source LLC
Chambersburg PA
CBHW060203290526
45789CB00003B/1138